To wish You a Year
of Happy Days.
from
Dorothy
Christmas /61.

HILLSIDE CHURCH

Where God creation doth present
  In its most lovely guise,
For Him are hearts and voices blent
  Who made all things arise.

DAVID HOPE

THE
FRIENDSHIP
BOOK

of

Francis Gay

A THOUGHT
FOR EACH DAY
IN 1962

D C. THOMSON & CO., LTD.   JOHN LENG & CO., LTD
LONDON · GLASGOW · MANCHESTER · DUNDEE

Let us be of good cheer,
remembering that the
misfortunes hardest to bear
are those which never come—

James Russell Lowell.

JANUARY

LORD, at the beginning of this new year I would dedicate myself anew.

I look back over the year which is past, and I see how far I have fallen short, how many golden opportunities for service I have neglected, how unworthy I have been, how mean, how slow to serve, how quick to lose my temper.

Forgive me, Lord. I am truly sorry.

And for the days that are ahead, the unspoiled days of this year of grace 1962, I pray Thee guide me, walk with me, speak with me by the way that I may feel my heart rejoice within me, strengthen me, preserve me, and point me ever to higher, nobler things.

Lord, I know I shall stumble and fall. I have always done so before. My deepest resolves have never saved me. I have begun well and finished badly. But these experiences shall not make me faint-hearted. I begin again now, not in my own strength, but in the faith that Thou wilt lift me up when I fall.

IF we were so minded, and so foolish, we could make ourselves very miserable by merely contemplating the certainty that in the days ahead we shall have a lot of trouble and a lot of disappointments and difficulties. Be as cheery as you will, as optimistic as you can, you *know* it's true.

But don't let's sit and weep. Let's make the best of the best and the least of the worst. Let's be brave and hopeful and adventurous—with some of the gay and gallant spirit of Robert Burns, who sang:—

> *He'll hae misfortunes great and sma',*
> *But aye a heart aboon them a'.*

WEDNESDAY—JANUARY 3.

WHEN last year dawned, I thought
  I'd do a lot of good—
And had not time slipped by so fast,
  I really think I should !

Now a new year is here,
  So while it still is new,
I'll do some of those kindnesses
  I meant last year to do !

THURSDAY—JANUARY 4.

FOR forty years John has been delivering newspapers.
    Every morning, seven days a week, he rises bright as a lark at half-past five and sets out round the streets with his bag of papers to call at 200 houses. In the evening he goes round with another bagful.

Nothing unusual in that, you say. Except that John is 67 years old and is blind. . . .

Honestly, can you imagine how any man can cope with blindness AND a daily newspaper round ? Yet John does just that and the remarkable thing is he needs no assistance. He even selects the papers and arranges them in strict order of delivery by himself in his shop.

Like me, you're bound to wonder how he can tell the difference between all the various papers. Well, somehow, John knows the feel of each newspaper. He just needs to touch a paper on the counter and he can tell you its name immediately.

It's the same with coins—he knows them by their weight and feel.

Here's Francis Gay saying well done, John ! It's a joy to hear of folk like you, who, through sheer determination and patience, have triumphed over one of the heaviest burdens a man has to carry.

FRIDAY—JANUARY 5.

I WONDER if you heard how a schoolboy helped the great Dr Schweitzer.

The boy, Robert Hill, had been reading about the work of Dr Schweitzer among the Africans. He was so impressed he told his father he was going to save part of his pocket money that week and buy a bottle of aspirins to send to the doctor's jungle hospital.

His father, a sergeant in the U.S. Air Force in Italy, laughed. "Why don't you see the Allied Commander and get him to fly them out for you?" he joked.

Believe it or not, that's just what Robert did! The Commander, busy man that he was, was touched by the boy's request and told others about it.

The news spread and soon offers of money and supplies for Dr Schweitzer's hospital poured in.

In the end, as well as Robert's aspirins, a whole planeload of medical supplies weighing four and a half tons was dispatched to Dr Schweitzer. Robert himself was on the plane with them.

No wonder the good doctor was almost speechless. "I never believed a child could do so much," he said, shaking his head.

To think it all started with one bottle of aspirins.

SATURDAY—JANUARY 6.

IT'S no use telling you not to worry.

Nothing I can say will stop you worrying—nothing anybody else can say, either. If you think you have something to worry about, you'll worry.

But I venture to suggest that you really ought now and then to examine your worries, deciding which worries are just not worth worrying about, and which are really big, urgent, worthwhile worries.

Then, if you *must* worry, worry about worthwhile worries!

SUNDAY—JANUARY 7.

FEAR not, little flock, for it is your Father's good pleasure to give you the kingdom.

MONDAY—JANUARY 8.

I'M not throwing stones at the Health Service. I am criticising nobody. I'm not comparing or contrasting today with yesterday. All I'm doing is remarking that I like the story of the little Scottish doctor who wore himself out soon after this century began, and would often excuse himself by saying : " I really must hurry along to surgery . . . I've such a lot of patients too poor to pay me anything, and I simply can't keep them waiting ! "

TUESDAY—JANUARY 9.

FIRST, I closed my eyes. Then I drew a sheet of paper towards me and felt for my pen.

I began to guide my pen along what I thought was a straight line. Next thing I knew the pen was off the paper. I tried to guess the place again, but I must have missed it by inches.

When I had struggled to the end of the first page I opened my eyes—and, goodness me, you should have seen the mess I had made of it !

I expect you're wondering what all this is about. I had just read one of the most remarkable letters that has ever come my way. It was written by Miss Nancy Cosgrove, who has been blind and bed-ridden for the last 11 years.

There were three pages to it, and I read every word as clearly as you're reading this.

A wonderful lady, Miss Cosgrove, who, in spite of her afflictions, counts her blessings and goes to all this trouble to write a letter.

WEDNESDAY—JANUARY 10.

WHEN sinks the sun, your short day done,
  And life is ebbing fast,
How sad to leave your cherished friends,
  To say farewell at last.

And yet how wonderful to know,
  Since God himself is love,
That when we part with friends below
  We meet with friends above.

THURSDAY—JANUARY 11.

HAVE you ever had a bag of pure gold turned into your coal cellar ?

Perhaps not—but let me tell you of some folk who, in a way, have had just that. They are customers of Archie Jack, the cheery coalman of Glasgow, and I couldn't do better than begin this tale with an incident that happened on a bitter night not so long ago.

It was around eight o'clock. A family of four were huddled round the dying embers of their fire when they found to their dismay there wasn't a scrap of coal left in the bunker.

As it turned out, Archie hadn't a single bag left in his store that night. But he couldn't leave the family without coal for the week-end, could he ? So he left his fireside, got out his lorry, and drove 12 miles to the depot for a fresh supply. Then he drove back—all to help one family that had forgotten to get in coal.

Another time a neighbour told Archie that a young mother with a new baby was without a fire—she'd no money to buy coal. Again Archie didn't hesitate. He humped up a bag for her—free !

Blessings on you, Archie ! I know you've been battling against ill-health for years, but I know also that your heart's in the right place.

FRIDAY—JANUARY 12.

EVER noticed what an amazing difference a bit of sunshine makes ?

Stand on a hillside on a day when the sky is clouded. Look over the plain below—so little colour there. But suppose the sun breaks through the clouds, what a miracle is performed, and how a hundred shades of green spring to life, and the stream becomes silver and trees and houses leap into life.

Don't go around in the home like a dull day— especially in this grim January weather. Carry some sunshine with you and so light up the lives of others.

SATURDAY—JANUARY 13.

IN the big hospital at Stracathro, Angus, a mother and daughter sit with downcast eyes at a little table.

For the most part they are silent, not even looking around, for it is already the third day they have sat at the same table, waiting, waiting.

Suddenly a phone rings. The women look up anxiously and watch George Paterson as he takes the message. Their eyes never leave his face as he replaces the phone. Then he walks towards them and bends over their table.

Quietly and kindly, he tells them the time has come for them to go to the ward where their loved one lies. He sees tears well into their eyes as they leave, for he knows as well as they do that this is the moment they have dreaded . . . their loved one is about to die.

It is years now since George took over the canteen in the hospital. Hundreds of relatives have found comfort there in the long hours of waiting, and to all of them George has shown the same compassion and understanding.

Thank you, George, on behalf of them all.

SUNDAY—JANUARY 14.

BLESSED are the poor in spirit : for theirs is the kingdom of heaven.

MONDAY—JANUARY 15.

THAT shrewd politician, William Cobbett, said last century · " From a very early age I had imbibed the opinion that it was every man's duty to do all that lay in his power to leave his country as good as he had found it."

It is a masterly understatement ; and it ought to come as a tremendous challenge to the youth of our own day, a challenge so to live and work and serve that their country is at least as good when they leave it as when they found it.

But why not leave it even better ?

TUESDAY—JANUARY 16.

MISS THOMSON is housebound and only able to move painfully to the door when anyone knocks, so the window has become her link with friends.

For years now I have been among those who are privileged to knock lightly on the window pane, then gently push it open.

In good weather, Miss Thomson can sit on one side of the window and gossip away with friends and neighbours on the other side.

When the weather is cold and she has to stay in bed, a word or two from the window lets her know she's not forgotten.

A neighbour slips the morning paper in the window. The coalman knocks on it to see if she needs coal.

Lonely old age asks very little in the way of enjoyment, but I bless the friendly window that means so much to Miss Thomson.

WEDNESDAY—JANUARY 17.

IF, discontented, you resent
Your own unhappy lot,
And wish you could be rid of all
The troubles you have got ,
Before your faith in God and man
You, in your folly, lose—
You might consider people who
Would gladly wear your shoes !

THURSDAY—JANUARY 18.

IT was a dreary walk to the prison gate; all the more dreary because night had fallen.

I saw the prison gate swing open a little as the visitors went in. First came two men, walking in step. Then a smartly dressed young woman went tapping past, her high heels beating a tattoo. Another woman went by—she was carrying a basket, and was hand-in-hand with a girl of perhaps six.

And all were going to prison. They were going to see somebody—perhaps somebody they loved.

Those two men ? Brothers of a criminal ? That young woman with the high heels ? Was it her sweetheart she was visiting ? The woman with the little girl . . . mother and daughter with permission to see Daddy ? A strange procession, surely fraught with more heartache than you and I can ever imagine.

It's one thing to be sent to prison. Quite another to be a loved one of somebody who is doing time . . What agonies of mind and heart are theirs, what undeserved disgrace and torment they suffer.

As I walked back towards the busy street I found myself offering a little prayer—not only for the prisoners—but for those loyal and loving men and women who, though innocent, deliberately choose to go to prison.

FRIDAY—JANUARY 19.

" THERE'S a hotwater bottle in the bed," the Lady of the House announced. " Drink this, and up you go ! "

" Not likely ! " said I. " It's half-past six, and I'm going to a meeting at seven—and I have some letters. . . ."

The Lady of the House was still holding out the glass. I made a fine show of being a man with a will of his own—and then crept up to bed, shivering.

How did the Lady of the House know I was feeling out of sorts ? And why did she bully me like that ? Could it be that love has a kind of second sight ?

Anyhow, those three days in bed did the trick !

SATURDAY—JANUARY 20.

GORDON is over 40, and for 20 years he has been confined to a wheelchair that he can't even propel.

What an existence you might think. Yet in the last 10 years Gordon has probably seen more of Glasgow than most folk there. This is how he does it.

Every morning he is pushed outside the gate of his home, and there he waits in his chair. Someone—a friend, perhaps, from down the road—slips behind the chair, and sets off with Gordon. Maybe he is only going a hundred yards, or maybe a mile, but wherever he is going, Gordon goes, too, in his chair.

What happens then? The friend simply leaves the chair in the street and bids Gordon a cheery good-bye. Gordon cheerfully waits until the next passer-by comes along—and, hey presto, he's off again ! And the thrilling bit of it all is that, for a helpless man in a wheelchair, he never knows where he is going or who he's going to meet !

So, remember, folk—if you see Gordon, give him a push ! It'll do you a world of good to meet him !

SUNDAY—JANUARY 21.

NOW the Lord of peace Himself give you peace at all times in all ways. The Lord be with you all.

MONDAY—JANUARY 22.

FROM getting up to going to bed tomorrow (or today) look out for the nice things.

You can be sure there will be all sorts of vexations and disappointments—take them in your stride, and keep both eyes and both ears open for the lovely things, the pleasant surprises, the friendly words, the happy tunes, the bright colours, the cheering thoughts which come your way, whether few or many.

The chances are that you'll be astonished at what a lot there is in any one day for which to be thankful.

TUESDAY—JANUARY 23.

ALTHOUGH Miss Mathieson had little, she had a genius for making life richer for many others.

It is years now since I first had a short letter from her, asking me to help someone in need and enclosing a little gift of money.

I heard from her often, and as we corresponded I was able to tell her that her gifts were finding their way like sunlight into many dark corners.

Even her last thoughts were for others. She knew she was nearing the end, and she asked a friend to send me £5 to carry on the good work even after she was gone.

How typical of her that other envelopes were handed over at the same time—with little gifts for an old people's club, for the blind and the disabled.

I'll miss her. It's hard to think she's gone. But it's wonderful to know that one who had so little helped so many she never even knew.

WEDNESDAY—JANUARY 24.

*THERE'S always far too much to do,
    Too little time to sit,
Too many worries, ills and cares
    For us to rest a bit.*

*But if we're thankful for each pause,
    And snatch each fleeting thrill,
Life's really not too bad—and we
    May keep on smiling still.*

THURSDAY—JANUARY 25.

MAYBE you think there's nothing very special in the story of Jackie.

Yet the more you know of him the more you will realise it's men like Jackie—quiet, decent, hard-working—who are the very backbone of our people.

For 54 years he has been a rabbit trapper and farm worker, with never a day out of work.

Loyal to the core, he fought—and was seriously wounded—in both wars. But it never occurred to him to ask his country for a pension.

He brought up four fine children, though he lost his wife when the youngest was only five.

In a year or two now he'll be thinking of retirement on no more than a widower's old age pension. It won't be much, but Jackie has other riches.

I can picture him when the time comes, sitting alone in his cottage. Beside him, on the couch, is a rug that's Sutherland tartan on one side and Mackenzie on the other. His wife made it by unpicking his two kilts, and it's a treasure from which he'll never part.

We spoke for quite a while, Jackie and I, and I don't think I've ever felt closer to the real character of Scotland.

FRIDAY—JANUARY 26.

REMEMBER the story of the nervous young man at a party ? He wanted to make a good impression, and to seem more intellectual than he was. " You'll know *Antony and Cleopatra* of course ? " somebody inquired.

The young man put on a smile. " Well," said he, " I know Antony, of course."

And in a famous 19th century novel we read : " We were none of us musical, though Miss Jenkyns beat time, out of time, by way of appearing to be so."

My advice is : Don't pretend to know what you don't or to be able to do what you can't.

SATURDAY—JANUARY 27.

IT'S eight years now since her husband died suddenly, leaving her with four young boys, one of them only a few months old.

How that young widow has managed to battle on since, no one knows, but battle on she has, in spite of weariness and loneliness. And those four boys of hers were a joy from the first, and still are.

Odd it is to realise that the youngest never knew his father. But, of course, he knows all about him from his mother and brothers.

One day recently, he realised it was his father's birthday. Without a word to anyone, he helped himself to pennies in his money-box and slipped out of the house to buy a few flowers and a birthday card.

Back home he put the flowers in a vase, wrote " With love " on the card, put both beside his father's photograph on the sideboard, and said earnestly——" Look, Dad, here's a card for you and some flowers for your birthday. I'm your son, Robert, and I'll never forget you !"

Do you wonder his mother feels proud?

THE FRIENDSHIP BOOK

THE lips of the wise disperse knowledge : but the heart of the foolish doeth not so.

HELEN had the job which always falls to the woman . going through her mother's effects shortly after the funeral.

Ever since she was a little girl Helen had felt that the bureau was very nearly sacred. Nobody knew its secrets except Mum. It was in the bureau she kept papers and documents, her rent book, and on occasion she brought out a spare £1 note.

The magic of that bureau touched Helen's life even after she was married and had three children, for Granny took to keeping sweets in the bureau, and brought them out mysteriously whenever her grandchildren came to see her.

Well, Granny's gone, and Helen had to go through that bureau. However, when Helen took her courage in both hands and opened its drawers, she found nothing very surprising—apart from one little photograph of a schoolgirl who looked a freak ; and at the back, in Granny's neat, precise hand—" Helen, aged 12 ; have kissed it many a time since it was taken."

No daughter ever loved her mother more than Helen. No daughter had ever been kinder to a mother. But with that faded photograph in her hands, Helen suddenly found herself weeping as she hadn't even wept at the funeral.

" Why didn't I love her more and do more for her?" she kept asking.

There was no reply. Even the grandfather clock in the corner was silent.

Maybe *you* are loved more than you know. . .

TUESDAY—JANUARY 30.

TRY to imagine it. . . .

You are standing any Sunday in the shadows of the great hall in Belmont Castle Eventide Home, Perthshire. Before you are sixty old people all joining together in worship. The last hymn has drawn to a close, and the minister raises his hands as he pronounces the benediction. There is a moment's silence . . . then softly the piano breaks into the lovely melody of the old psalm tune " Belmont "—the tune of the hymn, " By cool Siloam's shady rill."

The old folk sing just one verse—the last verse—of the hymn. They do this every Sunday, at the close of the service. They sing the same verse after meetings of the Men's Club and Woman's Guild. And when an old body passes to her rest, the funeral service ends with the same verse, just before she passes through the doors of the home for the last time.

I don't know how or when the tradition began. But I do know it has become a part of life at Belmont . . . a prayer asking only for the Lord's grace, that in their old age He may watch over them—

Dependent on Thy bounteous breath,
We seek Thy grace alone,
In childhood, manhood, age and death,
To keep us still Thine own.

WEDNESDAY—JANUARY 31.

WHEN the sun won't shine, when winds are chill,
When winter skies are grey,
Don't imagine you've a good excuse
For looking glum all day.
It is plain that that's the time when you
Should other folk beguile
With a merry song (though much is wrong)
And a sunny, sunny smile!

THE KEY

" Thank you, sir," and " If you please,"
My mother said were magic keys,
Smoothing life as we go by.
Perhaps they still are worth a try !

DAVID HOPE

THE WAY UP

One step, then another,
 You think they'll never stop!
Then, when you're 'most despairing,
 Gosh! You're at the top!

DAVID HOPE

FEBRUARY

LORD, I have a pretty long day ahead, and it won't be an easy day. There is much to do. There will be no end of worrying problems. It is going to be a long time before I go to bed, and I may be too tired then to say my prayers.

Therefore, here and now, before the bustle and rush of the day, I bow my head and pray for strength to do all I have to do, courage to be honest and to speak the truth, patience with things and people that exasperate; a graciousness and bigness of spirit enabling me to keep calm—and perhaps to grin—when it would be easy to lose my temper.

Do Thou bless me, Lord; and may I feel when the day is done I have never betrayed Thee. Amen.

HUSBANDS, they say, come in three varieties— prize, surprise and consolation.

It is a mystery why a fine, gentle woman should like a big, awkward, stubborn creature like a man.

If a woman flatters a man, she frightens him; if she doesn't, he gets tired. If a woman is the clinging-vine type, the man doubts if she has any brains. If she's independent and businesslike, he doubts if she has a heart. If she's pensive, he longs for someone gay. If she's brilliant, he'd like something docile.

If a wife is popular with other men, her husband gets jealous, and if she's not he doesn't like it. If a wife pleases her husband, he rarely says so. If she displeases him, he wastes no time letting her know.

By all the laws of mathematics, marriage is bound to be a failure, but most marriages are not—due to the wife!

SATURDAY—FEBRUARY 3.

MANY years ago, C. H. Kingsley wrote—" The men I have seen succeed best in life have always been cheerful and hopeful men, who went about their business with a smile on their faces."

So, remembering that success is not always measured in terms of hard cash, let's all go about our business today with a smile. It does make a difference, and who knows, perhaps we'll help others to smile too !

SUNDAY—FEBRUARY 4.

BE ye merciful, even as your Father is merciful.

MONDAY—FEBRUARY 5.

HAVE you ever thought how a little thing can change the whole course of your life?

There's James, for instance. It was a local holiday, the sun was shining brightly and, best of all, his grandad had promised to take him across the river on the ferry.

Alas, as grown-ups do, his grandfather met a crony on the way and stopped for a crack with him. The result was, of course, they missed the boat.

What a disappointment for an eight-year-old boy. Yet it was a blessing they missed that boat, for on the way over it sank with the loss of 32 lives.

Although it happened many years ago, James is still with us. I'm told he has been a living example to all around him.

And he still finds a way to serve, for he makes it his duty to guide the children into the church. It's a lovely picture, isn't it—the old man with the children.

Perhaps, many years ago, James told himself God had spared him for a good reason, and I'm sure no one could have been more faithful.

THE FRIENDSHIP BOOK

JOYCE KERR is in her twenties, and if you had known her a few years ago, you would have said she had all a girl could wish for. She was a teacher, she earned a good salary, and even ran a car.

Yet three years ago she gave all this up. She felt that behind the comfort and security there was something missing—something so important to her that her life would not be complete without it.

What was it? Simply that there were others in the world whose needs were so great someone had to help them. To do this, Joyce went back to college to begin the laborious task of learning the languages of pagan tribes in South America—languages that aren't even written down—so that she could be a missionary.

Recently she set off on her long journey into the jungle of Brazil to stay with people who have never heard of God. She will eat their frugal meals, and live with them in their primitive huts. And she will do this without pay of any kind.

How I admire this young girl for her sacrifice. Yet Joyce herself says she is giving up nothing, but instead is gaining everything.

God speed her in her chosen work.

IF you've a little house to keep
The winter winds away ;
If you've a tasty bite to eat,
And pleasant thoughts, each day.
If you can dream of yesterdays
As near the hearth you sit ;
If you've a neighbour who looks in,
And stays to chat a bit. . .
Though troubles you have by the score
You've SOMETHING to be thankful for !

THURSDAY—FEBRUARY 8.

I DOUBT if there is a happier man than David Bell, who lost his sight and hands in the last war.

Many years have gone since first I met him, bought an ounce of tobacco in his newly-opened shop, and handed in a one-pound note and received the correct change from a man who was still groping his way out of a black hell, still trying to get used to false hands, still a little bewildered by the difficulties of a wholly new life. I marvelled then at his courage.

How amazingly David Bell has used the minutes and years that have slipped by so quickly !

He has extended his activities to a life of service, through social welfare, hospital management, education. And he has studied so hard he is now able to put M.A. and B. (Comm.) after his name !

All of us would be the richer if we could take the worst and give our best as he has given it.

FRIDAY—FEBRUARY 9.

MR MATHER is 92, and for the last 53 years he has been a church elder.

A grand record, you may say, and the congregation thought so too. So they decided to say thank you for all he had done for the church over the years.

A goodly sum was collected and Mr Mather was asked to choose the gift he wanted. There were plenty of suggestions, and I'm told one was a comfortable easy chair for the fireside. What could be better than that for a man in his nineties?

But did Mr Mather want an easy chair? Dear me, no ! Believe it or not, he chose a lawnmower, spade, garden fork and wheel-barrow, for it seems there's no keener gardener than Mr Mather—even at 92.

You're a marvel, sir. I wish more of us had your lively spirit and outlook on life !

SATURDAY—FEBRUARY 10.

A FEW old proverbs to think about :—
  He loseth nothing that loseth not God.
Nothing is impossible to a willing heart.
Right wrongs no man.
Say well is good, but do well is better.
Nothing improves so much with keeping as temper.

SUNDAY—FEBRUARY 11.

AS ye would that men should do to you, do ye also to them likewise.

MONDAY—FEBRUARY 12.

LET me tell you about Miss Mary Anderson. She was a helpless invalid who couldn't walk. For years she had been practically a prisoner in her room.

Almost her only outing was when she went to church in her wheelchair. Someone carried her to the chair and a boy called to push her to and from the church.

But one Sunday morning a surprising thing happened. As the boy steered Miss Anderson's chair round some pedestrians, he didn't notice he was too close to the wall. Suddenly there was a bump—and poor Miss Anderson was tipped out !

It seemed to be the last straw, for when she was taken off to the infirmary there were folk who didn't expect her to come out again.

But they were wrong ! Not only did the indomitable Miss Anderson come out—she actually walked out, on a pair of crutches ! Now she has thrown away her crutches, too, and she's walking unaided for the first time for years.

Isn't it remarkable that this new, exciting life has been opened up for Miss Anderson—all because she fell out of her wheelchair?

TUESDAY—FEBRUARY 13.

MRS NICOL is almost eighty—and I don't think I've ever heard of anyone who has had a harder life.

Her husband died when he was only twenty-eight. She was left with two sons and three daughters, and another little boy was born three months later.

God alone knows how she managed to keep her home going and her family clothed and fed. Yet not one of them ever knew what it was to be hungry or cold.

Then, to crown all, when Mrs Nicol was 55, she took into her home a girl only six weeks old, to bring up as her own !

Now this remarkable mother has the reward she richly deserves. Her three daughters are happily married, and so is the girl she adopted. Her eldest son was awarded the B.E.M. recently, and the other two are also doing well. She has 18 grandchildren and 12 great-grandchildren—and I know no family could love their granny more, for one of them has told me all about her.

What's her secret? I can only guess . . . perhaps when God took away her husband, He gave her the courage to bear the burden—and the patience to look into the future with trust.

WEDNESDAY—FEBRUARY 14.

YOU loved the one you've lost ? Well then,
    How can you help but weep ?
Must not the kindest words of cheer
    Seem trivial and cheap ?

But if the one you loved loved you,
    Though you are stricken now,
Be sure that spirit longs to see
    You smile again somehow.

Thursday—February 15.

MR OTLEY was sitting by the beach at Filey Bay, on a sunny afternoon, and beside him was a stranger—an elderly lady.

Soon the two began to chat. Her name was Miss Amy Jackson, and she came from a village in Yorkshire.

All her life, it seems, she had worked in a mill, helping to give her brothers and sisters a start. Then, when they were all away, she stayed on at home to look after her old father and mother. Now they had passed on, and she was alone.

That's why this ordinary day trip to the seaside meant so much to her. Why, she said, she had never had a proper holiday in her life.

Mr Otley was touched, and there and then he told her he had a friend with a hotel nearby—and if she liked she could have a holiday there—free !

So she came back in the autumn and she brought with her a paint-box and brushes, for all her life she had found pleasure in painting, though she had never had any tuition. Other guests in the hotel were charmed by her work and promptly bought her pictures.

Miss Jackson was so encouraged that when she returned home she held an exhibition of her work, and now, although she's nearly 70, she's overwhelmed with orders, and her life has taken on a new, exciting meaning !

All because of a chance meeting at the seaside.

Friday—February 16.

EVEN if the doctor does not give you a year, even if he hesitates about a month, make one brave push and see what can be accomplished in a week.

ROBERT LOUIS STEVENSON.

SATURDAY—FEBRUARY 17.

I SAW this verse on a printed card in the home of a friend. He tells me it has always been a help and inspiration to him :—

Heaven is not reached at a single bound ;
But we build the ladder by which we rise
From the lowly earth to the vaulted skies,
And we mount to its summit round by round.

SUNDAY—FEBRUARY 18.

I AM come a light into the world, that whosoever believeth on Me may not abide in the darkness.

MONDAY—FEBRUARY 19.

NEARLY 20 years ago a little girl, Anne, began singing lessons. Most mothers would have had the reward of hearing their daughters sing, but the sad thing is Anne's mother never could. She was quite deaf.

Anne grew up and became a lovely singer and her chance came when she was asked to sing the soprano solos in Handel's " Messiah." How her mother's joy must have been tinged with regret at not being able to share her daughter's triumph.

But worse was to happen. A few days before the great day, Anne's mother died suddenly. . . .

That night, as the girl tried to fight back the tears, a friend of the family said, " Of course, you'll not be taking part in the ' Messiah ' now?"

Anne turned and replied quietly, " Yes, I will. For the first time Mum will be able to hear me !"

Anne did sing—and those who heard her said she never sang better. When she came to " I know that my Redeemer liveth," it was the song not of a broken-hearted girl, but of a young woman secure in the knowledge of her triumphant faith.

WEAPONS

Here men found a refuge
From the arrows and the spears :
But love alone will armour us
Against the hostile years.

DAVID HOPE

A WINTER WALK

Oh, what is so fine
As a walk in the snow
When the hard winter sunshine
Puts the wood in a glow!

You breathe a new air
  With each step as you go.
Oh, what is so rare
  As a walk in the snow!

DAVID HOPE

THE BUILDERS

In my mind I see them yet,
  The men who laboured here.
Arch and pillar firm they set
  To stand a thousand year.

Of joy and grief they had their store,
  Shared our brief earthly story,
But in their eyes a vision bore
  Of faith's deep inward glory.

DAVID HOPE

MY old friend, John Forbes, is still a lad at heart—humorous, whimsical, delightful.

Passing his house one Saturday afternoon I noticed he was busy in his garage. John has no car, but the garage is useful—his wife (he says) can throw all the lumber, including her hubby, into it, and so keep the house tidy.

John was hard at work mending a broken deck-chair. He's a handyman, and was doing the job very seriously when I looked in.

" Go away, go away," he ordered in a most cantankerous manner. " Don't interrupt me. Urgent. Must get it done at once."

" Get what done?" I inquired, for I know old John.

" This deck-chair. Must get it mended in double quick time. Not a moment to lose."

" You're not likely to be using a deck-chair. . . ."

John sniffed. "Little you know," he retorted. " There's only March and April and then it will be May, and before we've turned round it will be the middle of July, and how's my wife going to watch me cutting the lawn if she hasn't a deck-chair to sit on ! Away with you !"

I did not away. I stayed on and chatted with old John Forbes.

WEDNESDAY—FEBRUARY 21.

THE road's uphill for you, but sure
*   You'll reach the top at length ;*
The way is steep and rough, but friend,
You'll find the needed strength.
So climb and sing and pray and strive
In spite of thorn and stone,
For if God be your guide, why then
You do not climb alone !

THURSDAY—FEBRUARY 22.

I SUPPOSE there are times when all of us find our faith is sorely tried.

In times like these I think of Charlotte Elliott. Miss Elliott lived in a comfortable house in Brighton last century. Perhaps because of the ill-health that had beset her for years, she found herself asking if there really was a God who cared.

One day, after a sleepless night, she lay tired and weary. All her doubts and fears came crowding in about her—and there and then she resolved to set down on paper what her faith really meant to her, in the hope that it would help her.

And so from a suffering and anxious heart came the hymn, " Just as I am, without one plea "—the hymn that has brought hope to people all over the world.

Just as I am, though tossed about
With many a conflict, many a doubt,
Fightings and fears within, without
—O Lamb of God, I come.

FRIDAY—FEBRUARY 23.

I KNOW a young man—not yet 24—who doesn't have to get up pretty early on dark, chilly mornings. I have to tumble out in order to catch a bus . . . not this lucky young man who can lie abed when there's an east wind blowing or the fog hangs around the houses or there's a touch of frost.

Lucky young man, I repeat.

Or unlucky ? For this young man was telling me last Sunday that he would give anything, anything he has, to be able to get up, wash and dress, and run to catch a bus !

So, perhaps after all, I'm the lucky one . . . there's nothing wrong with my legs !

SATURDAY—FEBRUARY 24.

WHEN I was on my way home from the office one afternoon recently I realised that the Lady of the House has been having rather a rough time of it lately—a distant relative has been on the sick-list, and my wife has been doing all she could. So I popped into a shop, and bought some daffodils and tulips.

It seems that when the Lady of the House was shopping she told herself I had had quite a few worries, so she popped into a shop and bought a few flowers.

The two bunches—mingled together—have cheered both of us no end !

SUNDAY—FEBRUARY 25.

O KEEP my soul, and deliver me : let me not be ashamed, for I put my trust in Thee.

MONDAY—FEBRUARY 26.

GEORGE CURRIE was a roadman and for 20 years it was his special job to look after a bit of hilly road. It could be very tricky, especially in winter.

That's where George came in. During these 20 years, every bus driver knew the road would be safe. For George thought nothing of getting up at two in the morning and setting out to clear and sand the hill.

George didn't have to get up. Nobody ordered him to. And, of course, he got no extra money for what he did. But he earned something more than money—the gratitude and respect of every bus driver on the road.

Now George has retired—and the bus drivers haven't forgotten him. When word went round that he would be leaving soon, they got together and presented him with a wallet and twelve pound notes.

A humble man in a humble job. Yet George went about it with dignity and faithfulness.

TUESDAY—FEBRUARY 27.

IF you're ever tempted to feel sorry for yourself—
read on.

This is the story of Mrs Annie Reilly and her son,
Claude.

It began four weeks after Claude was born, when it
became clear he wasn't as well as he should have been.
When he was only four he was moved to hospital—
and he hasn't been away from a hospital bed since.

Yet here is the splendid thing. No matter where
he has been during these years, his mother has visited
him every Saturday without a break. . . .

It began when, as a young mother, she went to
see Claude, who was little more than a baby. As the
years passed she saw him grow from boy to youth
and youth to man. And with each visit, too, she could
see that her son was gradually growing more helpless
as his feet, legs, hands and arms became paralysed.
Now, as if his burden were not heavy enough, he has
been told he is going blind.

Many a man would have lost interest in what is
left of life, but not Claude Reilly. In spite of forty
years of pain in a world bounded by four walls, he
can still smile. He would be the first to admit he is
able to do so only because of the devotion of his
mother, who has always been there when he needed her.

WEDNESDAY—FEBRUARY 28.

MAYBE it's wishful thinking,
Maybe the coldest days
Are coming yet to try us
With snow and icy ways !
But I was sure this morning
That bird-song brought the day,
And felt—if prematurely—
That Spring was on the way !

MARCH

I DON'T know who wrote these words, but what a
world of wisdom they hold :—

I'd rather see a sermon than hear one any day ;
I'd rather you would walk with me than merely show
the way ;
The eye is a better pupil and more willing than the ear ;
Fine counsel is confusing, but example's always clear.
I soon can learn to do it if you let me see it done ;
I can watch your hands in action but your tongue too
fast may run.
The lectures you deliver may be very wise and true ;
But I'd rather get my lessons by observing what you do;
I may not understand the high advice you give,
But there's no misunderstanding how you act and how
your live.

Friday—March 2.

A SMILE costs nothing, but gives much.

It enriches them who receive, without making
poorer those who give.

It takes but a moment, yet the memory of it might
last for ever.

A smile creates happiness in the home, fosters
goodwill in business, and is the sign of friendship.

It brings rest to the weary, cheer to the discouraged,
sunshine to the sad, and is nature's best antidote to
trouble.

Yet a smile cannot be bought, begged, borrowed
or stolen ; for it is something of no value to anyone
unless it is given away.

Some people are too tired to give you a smile. Give
them one of yours. No one needs a smile so much as
he who has none to give.

SATURDAY—MARCH 3.

AN elderly man happened to be talking to me one day, and I remember especially one thing he said. I rather think I shall keep on remembering it. Smilingly, he told me that life always brings suffering and trouble and worry and disappointment.

Then he added : " But every day has a few minutes in it, at least, when we can enjoy ourselves. The thing to do is to enjoy our enjoyment when it comes and as long as it lasts. You may be hurrying to the dentist, but if you see a very pretty girl, well, enjoy looking at her for five seconds, even though the pain almost drives you frantic. That's the secret !"

SUNDAY—MARCH 4.

WHO is wise and understanding among you? let him shew by his good life his works in meekness of wisdom.

MONDAY—MARCH 5.

I LIKE the story about the laddie who was cleaning a shop window. He hadn't left school very long ago. He was not an expert at the job. With his steps and his pail and his washleather he was doing his best, but wondering all the time why the window didn't look very much cleaner. It was no use, that shop window just wouldn't shine as it ought to have done.

Fortunately a passerby paused, looked at the window and at the laddie, and whispered confidentially " I'd try cleaning the inside, sonny, if I were you !"

My only comment is this : If a lot of things are wrong about your life, maybe instead of altering this and that it would be a good idea to clean up the inside. Perhaps a cheerier, braver, sweet spirit might transform your drab world into something a bit like heaven !

THE FRIENDSHIP BOOK

SEVENTEEN years ago, young William McAlpine
was a builder in Larbert.

With the war over, he decided to offer himself in
the work of rebuilding devastated London. So he said
good-bye to his folk in Larbert, gave up his place in
the kirk choir and set out for the South.

As he worked on the ruined buildings, he sang—
and folk passing by often stopped and listened to his
fine voice. Then one day, a stranger was so struck by
its beauty that she offered to help him have his voice
trained by the best teachers.

He jumped at the chance, and since then the voice
of William McAlpine has become world famous. He
has sung in the opera houses of Europe and concert
halls of London. Yet he has never forgotten the time
he sat in the choir at Larbert Old Church.

So it was fitting that recently he was in his old seat
again. Few of the congregation knew he was there.

But in the middle of the service, he stepped forward
and sang Mendelssohn's moving aria—" If with all
your heart you truly seek Me. . . ." He sang it as
though it was, indeed, a prayer and when the last
notes died away there were tears in the eyes of many.

How much I admire the great singer who is humble
enough to come back to his old kirk choir.

YOUR job is hard? Each day seems long?
You've worries quite a lot?
There's this and that as wrong as wrong,
What troubles you have got!
But if in all the world ONE heart
Is filled with love for you,
How cheerily you plod along,
How bravely battle through!

THURSDAY—MARCH 8.

I WAS talking with a young and pretty nurse in a home for folk who are not quite sane. I was sorry when she had (as she said) to run away and look after her dears.

Those dears did not look very attractive. All were abnormal and difficult, yet that young nurse seemed to love them. She chatted away. She cajoled. Now and then she was firm. Often she laughed.

Later I said, " How can you do it?"

Again that bright smile and twinkle in her eyes. " Oh," said she, " it's because I'm thankful I'm not like them !"

It was said lightly—playfully. But I came away thinking that perhaps it was just about the whole truth. She was thankful for the wonderfully precious gifts of sanity and normality . . . so thankful that she was glad to minister to those less fortunate, share their strange and unsatisfying world, and help them along the dark road.

Bless you, nurse !

FRIDAY—MARCH 9.

A MINISTER was telling me that he had heard two remarks quite recently.

On a bus he couldn't help hearing one woman saying to another : " That's the minister whose church we go to."

And when passing some children playing in the street, one child called to the others : " There's the minister who comes to our church."

Of the two, the little boy came nearer the truth ; for no matter where we may be, our church is OUR church ; so why don't we go there more often, play a greater part in church life, make sure OUR church flourishes ?

JUST THE JOB!

Did you hear me barking
To Master and the Missis?
I simply had to show them
What a splendid idea this is!

DAVID HOPE

THE RIVER'S SONG

Happy the folk who have their homes
  Beside a river singing,
To orchard and to garden tales
  Of far-off mountains bringing.
There's glory in the dews of dawn,
  The woods bow in their graces,
But, oh, for me the river's song
  As to the sea it races.

DAVID HOPE

SATURDAY—MARCH 10.

ONE evening in 1866 a young medical student, training for the foreign mission field, was about to leave a mission meeting. A poorly-clad boy came forward shyly. " Will you let me sleep by the fire here?" he asked.

The student looked down kindly. " What'll your mother say when you don't go home?" he asked.

" I've no home to go to," said the boy, " and no mother." Later he took the student to London Docks, where scores of homeless boys were trying to sleep crouched under tarpaulins, in boxes and barrels.

As the student lay in bed that night, he couldn't forget the plight of the boys. Next evening he went to another meeting, and the chairman invited him to speak on the work he intended to do as a missionary. But instead, he began to tell of the homeless boys at the docks. The whole pitiful story tumbled out in an impassioned flood. When at length he finished there was a hush, and a servant girl went forward with an envelope. " It's my savings," she said. " Use them to help these boys." Inside were 27 farthings.

In a flash, the student knew he had been called to minister to the homeless waifs he had seen.

His name was Dr Thomas Barnardo.

Twenty-seven farthings—yet I believe all the gold in the world would be too small to measure the worth of the work they helped to begin.

SUNDAY—MARCH 11.

AND Jesus, when He was baptized, went up straight-way from the water : and lo, the heavens were opened unto Him, and He saw the Spirit of God descending as a dove, and coming upon Him ; and lo, a voice out of the heavens, saying, This is My beloved Son, in whom I am well pleased.

MONDAY—MARCH 12.

WHAT a lot of crooked thinking there is, isn't there?
Some people over-eat, but are not at all troubled about digging their graves with their teeth. Why should they be? They take a few pills or a powder or two . . . and, therefore, their interiors are *bound* to be all right !

Some people go elbowing their way regardless of old or young, and when they bump into somebody they snap, " Sorry !" and go blundering on. Their argument would be—" Well, what does it matter if I knocked you into the gutter? I apologised, didn't I?"

And some folk break just about every commandment there is—and get away with it because they give a donation to charity !

What it all adds up to is this—it doesn't matter if you do wrong as long as you do something right. You can be bad one way if you're good in another.

Perhaps if we realise we're living in this unsatisfactory way we'll try to do something about it and stop deceiving ourselves.

TUESDAY—MARCH 13.

I KNOW a woman who did literally lend her last shilling.

I know a man who took the blame to save his brother from disgrace.

I know a bedridden girl who cheers the neighbours with her singing.

I know a woman who will not hear one unkind word about the husband who has left her for another woman.

I know an old granny who is " mother " to two unwanted children. . . .

The badness in this world grieves me. The goodness—often found in unlikely places—humbles me.

WEDNESDAY—MARCH 14.

WHEN everything goes right for you,
And you seem in luck's way,
How easy then to keep your faith
And sing a song each day.
But he has faith and she is brave
Who, when the sun has gone,
With patient feet and spirit sweet,
Keep ever pressing on.

THURSDAY—MARCH 15.

SOME people have a genius for friendliness.

A minister I heard about has had to retire for reasons of health. He found himself, therefore, on a new housing estate where he knew nobody.

After getting things fixed up in the house, the minister took a look at the " garden," and wondered if the wilderness would ever blossom.

Obviously it wouldn't, unless somebody removed the half-bricks, dug up the virgin earth, and planted seeds. So, sleeves rolled up, he buckled to.

Soon, along came a schoolboy and stood watching. The minister, being what he is, grinned, spoke, went indoors for lemonade and a bun, and made a friend in twenty minutes. His ally started picking up bricks.

Presently, another boy appeared and began to help . . . and another, all charmed by the good man's smile and friendly manner—and perhaps attracted by the empty glasses on the wall !

In the end, eight workers, including the minister, made a game of clearing the garden—such a game that everybody was sorry when bedtime came round.

But the minister didn't bargain for what happened next morning. There was a timid knock at the door ; and when his wife opened it, there stood a small girl. " Please," she said, " can your man come out to play?"

FRIDAY—MARCH 16.

HOLD on a bit longer, folk.

You have weathered the winter—and a strange winter it's been—and now it is March, maybe as cold as ever, and perhaps even colder, but if only you'll hold on a bit longer you'll come through to warmer and sunnier days.

I like the story of the gallant old lady who, suffering from bronchitis, was told by her doctor to take care because March winds could be dangerous. " Oh," snapped she, " I'm no fool, doctor. I've managed along all through the worst of the winter—I'm going to enjoy summer if I can."

That's the spirit !

And, however unkind the weather may be at the moment or will be the week after next, let's remind ourselves that the days are longer ; that the sun's climbing higher in the sky ; that birds are singing and building nests, and flowers appearing in the gardens and the children beginning to play out of doors after school.

Hold on a bit longer . . . the kindlier days are only just ahead.

SATURDAY—MARCH 17.

YOU'VE got to hand it to the Irish !

Did you hear about the traveller in Ireland who noticed that a certain railway station had two clocks on one platform, each pointing to a different time ?

This so annoyed the traveller that he demanded of a porter : " Why in the world have two clocks each pointing to a different time ? "

The porter's hackles were up at once. " And what use would it be having two clocks both pointing to the same time ? " he asked !

SUNDAY—MARCH 18.

BE subject therefore unto God ; but resist the devil, and he will flee from you.

MONDAY—MARCH 19.

THERE'S a go-head young Scotsman who keeps on his desk at the office a saying in a frame only a few inches square.

He confessed recently that he was not sure who first said or wrote the famous words—some say it was Elbert Hubbard, others that it was Ralph Waldo Emerson. " It doesn't matter much," declared this go-ahead young Scotsman. " The fact remains that it's a challenge."

The quotation is:— " If a man write a better book, preach a better sermon or make a better mouse trap than his neighbour, though he build his house in the woods, the world will make a beaten path to his door."

TUESDAY—MARCH 20.

I HEAR that Peter, aged 24, flew to South Africa recently.

It meant leaving his widowed mother alone at home —and Mum has always been nervous (as she herself expresses it) about aeroplanes. Travelling all those miles by air was just an exciting adventure to Peter— the young university student who means to get on.

But Peter knew that Mum would worry, so after he had said " Good-bye," and given Mum a kiss, he grinned all over his round face, and added : " Now don't start thinking up things to think about."

It was droll yet good advice, wasn't it? And it might be said to you . . . anything may happen, much can go wrong, tomorrow is forbidding : but don't start thinking up things to think about.

WEDNESDAY—MARCH 21.

WHEN you are old and short of breath,
And slow to move about,
When days are dull and nights are long
Because you can't go out,
How nice to sit before the fire
And dream of days gone by
When grass was brighter green, somehow,
And sunnier the sky.
How nice, at eventide, to hear
The voices loved in yesteryear!

THURSDAY—MARCH 22.

THERE was no answer to my knock—so I did as I had been told. I pushed open the letter-box, felt for the chain I'd been assured was dangling there, drew it up, and with the key on the end of it I opened the door—and stepped in to meet the gallant Mrs Dewar.

Her two boys were only eleven and three years old when she first became ill. She managed to carry on for a few years, and when at last she had to remain in bed, her husband, James, a postman, took over. At first, Mrs Dewar told him what to do from her bed, and so he was able to bring up the children, look after his wife, and do his day's work as well.

Friends and neighbours are, of course, wonderfully kind, and all know the secret of the letter-box that I was allowed to share. The coalman, grocer's boy, laundry boy . . . they're in the secret, too. The coalman even sees the fire's well banked up before he goes.

Mrs Dewar doesn't expect she'll ever get out and about again. Yet she counts her blessings—the blessings of a devoted husband, family and friends. And, not least, the blessing of a chain and key rattling through the letter-box, telling her she is not forgotten.

<u>FRIDAY—MARCH 23.</u>

ONCE upon a time there was a man who got it into his head he was unlucky.

In the first place, he was wrecked on a desert island. That was bad enough. But he was without a friend, and it was at the beginning of the wet season. He salvaged nothing from the wreck except a box of matches—so he had to work and sleep in the open air, which meant being wet most of the time.

At last, however, he managed to build himself a hut to keep the rain off ; and there he dried his matches until one day he managed to strike one, and at long last have a fire for heat and cooking.

But fate was against him. In the night a gust of wind blew flames from his fire over the hut, and his shelter (and his box of matches) were destroyed.

Was ever a man unluckier?

But that isn't the end of the story. With the crack of dawn came a boat . . . and he was rescued.

" It was the fire we saw burning in the night," the captain explained. " We thought the island was un-inhabited, and when we saw the blaze we turned back to investigate."

In other words, folk, the worst—the very worst—turned out the very best !

<u>SATURDAY—MARCH 24.</u>

DR MANDELL CREIGHTON wrote these maxims last century, but I have always found them true, especially in the world of today.

Character is revealed in crises. The great marks of character are teachableness and a capacity for growth.

We cannot improve the world further than we improve ourselves.

Nothing is so pernicious as mere diffusion. What you need is a definite object and perseverance.

SUNDAY—MARCH 25.

WHOSOEVER therefore shall humble himself as this little child, the same is the greatest in the kingdom of heaven. And whoso shall receive one such little child in My name receiveth Me.

MONDAY—MARCH 26.

WHEN I caught sight of the small, stooping figure, I pulled up, opened the car window and called, " Care for a lift?"

" No, thanks," replied Andrew—eighty if he's a day. " I'm on my way to the cemetery."

" Going to look at a grave?"

" Not me," he replied. " Going as far as the gate, then turning back."

" But why?"

" Man, man," he said, " you don't know how thankful I am I can go to the cemetery—and come away again !"

TUESDAY—MARCH 27.

" LONELY ? " Miss Forbes echoed when the Lady of the House was visiting her for the first time. " Oh, no. Not at all. You might think a body who is bedridden on the third floor would be lonely, and I can quite understand you imagining it.

" But you're wrong, my dear. Nurse looks in every day. My neighbour across the stair pops in with something to eat at least three times a day—she's an angel, of course. Lots of children drop in for a chat— and I make them laugh." She paused. Then she added with a wonderful smile : " Oh, and I mustn't forget that nobody passes my door without shouting a greeting."

It takes very little to make some folk thankful.

THE FRIENDSHIP BOOK

*A*T *the bottom of my garden,*
Where the fairies ought to be,
A merry bird is singing
In a lilac tree.

How he warbles in the sunshine,
With a rainbow on his wing !
And surely he's announcing :
Once again it's SPRING !

THURSDAY—MARCH 29.

I WAS in court the other day.

I looked and listened. And I was struck by the number of people who had been trying to get something to which they had no right—youths after cash in a shop, somebody who had defrauded his boss, a man who had hit another man and run off with his wallet. And what made me think hard was this—not one of the law-breakers was poor.

Has it occurred to you, I wonder, that fifty or a hundred years ago no end of people robbed because they were so poor they (or their children) were very near to starving? It is never right to steal—but you somehow feel inevitably inclined to be lenient to the poor creature who is hungry.

Today, however, nine times out of ten those who steal or cook the books are never satisfied with what they have. Having much (by the standards of last century) they want more.

And, of course, you and I can do precious little about it. But those of us who have children can, I suggest, try to teach our young folk the value of money, how to earn it honestly, how to spend it wisely, how to be master of it rather than allowing it to master (and, therefore, ruin) us.

FRIDAY—MARCH 30.

FRANCIS GAY proudly lifts his hat to one of the smallest villages in Scotland.

It's the village of Temple, Midlothian.

Some 15 years ago when a well-loved villager died, Mr Baillie, the postmaster, started a beautiful little custom in the village. He went to *every* door in the community, collecting for a village wreath.

It was made of flowers grown in the village and it became Temple's token of respect to its own.

At every death since in the village either Mr Baillie or a helper has made the same round and everyone has contributed to this unique symbol of fellowship.

Often, of course, more money is collected than is required . . . the balance is then gifted to a charity in memory of the one who has gone.

Not much, to be sure, but in its own way a precious and lovely gift indeed.

SATURDAY—MARCH 31.

WHEN somebody has hurt you deeply, and the wrong can never be put right, what do you do about it ?

You can be angry, but it will do no good. You can perhaps take legal proceedings and get some sort of financial satisfaction. But it does not restore the happiness lost. You can drink heavily, and forget— but there's only one end to that.

Friend, you have your choice. If you let this terrible burden break you, you'll live miserably. If somehow you are brave enough not to allow your just complaint to eat into your heart, you will find that there has never yet been a gallant man or woman who kept on without one day realising that unlooked-for compensations were enriching and comforting them.

APRIL

Sunday—April 1.

AND Jesus came to them and spake unto them, saying, All authority hath been given unto Me in heaven and on earth.

Monday—April 2.

JIMMY ran away to sea as a lad and was torpedoed in the First World War. Afterwards he had his own business as a contractor and bus owner, and a good job he made of it, working hard for his wife and two boys.

But, alas, the flash of the torpedo had done more harm than Jimmy knew.

Slowly his sight began to go until at last he was blind. Even so, he struggled on for 12 years before he had to give up.

It was then, when things seemed blackest, that a new door swung open for Jimmy.

He went to the Institute for the Blind in Middlesbrough and was asked what he thought he could do. For long Jimmy had had a secret wish to be a joiner —and, blind as he was, a joiner he became.

How long it took him to master the tools I do not know. But I can tell you this. If you visit the office of the institute you will see the counter and cabinets and cupboards and other office furniture which were all made by Jimmy, and I would defy you to tell it was the work of a blind man whose only special tool is a ruler with shallow notches to mark half inches and deeper ones to mark inches.

I know nothing can make up for blindness, especially when it comes in middle age, but as I watched Jimmy at work I marvelled at yet another of life's compensations.

TUESDAY—APRIL 3.

IT has happened many a time before—I have walked into a hotel bedroom and found there a Bible.

But this time I had a more careful look and in a preface to the Book itself I read it was one of over 30 million Bibles and New Testaments that have been placed in hotel rooms or given away to folk who might never have owned a Bible otherwise.

Since last century, it seems, the Gideons, an association of professional and business men, have been quietly doing this special job for God—just making sure that the Bible is at hand in tens of thousands of hotel bedrooms.

It is, I think a happy thing that the Gideons should print a sort of " key " to the Bible.

In the Bible I found in my hotel bedroom last week there were these words :—Where to find help when *afraid* (Hebrews 13, verses 5-8) ; *anxious* (Isaiah 43, verses 1-3) ; *discouraged* (I. Corinthians 15, verses 57-58) ; *leaving home* (Luke 15, verses 11-32) ; *in sorrow* (Romans 8, verses 34-39).

Good work, Gideons . . . long may you keep on putting the word of God in places where folk can read it when the door is shut !

WEDNESDAY—APRIL 4.

" *IT puzzles me," a thrush remarked,*
Conversing with a lark,
" *Why humans on an April day*
Look glum when in the park.
You'd think," said he, " they'd shout or dance
Because at last it's spring.
How odd they don't do as we do,
And sing and sing and sing !"
" *That," said the lark, " is no surprise :*
They're clever, chum . . . but are they wise?"

THE FRIENDSHIP BOOK

THURSDAY—APRIL 5.

WHEN Granny Chalmers was 70 her son's wife died. He was left with seven of a family to bring up, the youngest a child of only two.

Although she had brought up a family of her own and could have been forgiven for wishing a quiet retirement, Granny cared for them until she saw the youngest boy into long trousers.

What kept her going all these years? Faith. Whenever she felt low she thought of the old hymn, " Abide with me," and she knew she was not alone.

Now, at 90, and with her sight gone, she isn't able to get about, so the church choir sometimes goes to sing for her on Sunday evenings, and they always remember to sing " her hymn," as she calls it.

It has become her prayer—and I cannot think of a finer one for a lonely old lady.

" Abide with me, fast falls the eventide ;
The darkness deepens, Lord, with me abide. . . ."

FRIDAY—APRIL 6.

I WONDER if I dare pass on a story I found in an American magazine.

Seems that during a church outing a motor coach overturned and all the women in it were killed. Of course, their souls flew straight to heaven, but St Peter had to find accommodation for them for a week till suitable arrangements could be made inside the pearly gates. So the ladies went below. . . .

Five days later Satan telephoned St Peter—" Hi, you up there ! For goodness' sake look sharp about building that annexe. I must be rid of these women before tomorrow morning. What with their garden parties, jumble sales, hot-pot suppers, concerts and bazaars, they're only fifty dollars short of air-conditioning this place !"

SATURDAY—APRIL 7.

I CAME across this passage of Milton's in my reading the other day.

" In those vernal seasons of the year, when the air is calm and pleasant, it were an injury and sullenness against nature not to go out and see her riches and partake in her rejoicing."

So I took the Lady of the House out for a walk on a lovely spring afternoon, and we both had to agree that Milton was perfectly correct.

SUNDAY—APRIL 8.

THE heavens declare the glory of God ; and the firmament sheweth His handywork.

MONDAY—APRIL 9.

I THINK that if you had told David Stiven ten years ago that one day he'd be a minister he would have laughed in disbelief.

Granted, he was a son of the manse—but when he finished his studies at Oxford University and set sail for Canada, it was to a good position in business.

For ten years David worked in his chosen career, and succeeded. Yet, as time passed, he realised his life was meant for finer things. So, without counting the cost, he willingly gave up his position in business and his prospects, and began to study for the ministry.

Today David Stiven is an ordained minister. Soon he will be leaving Canada to go to Africa, where he will work as a missionary among those who know little or nothing of the God who created them.

How appropriate all this is, for David's father is minister of Iona—the island to which Saint Columba came as a missionary 1400 years ago,.

Godspeed to you, David.

TUESDAY—APRIL 10.

I WISH I had known Mrs Gibson.

I am told she was a grand old lady, but it was easy to see, though her face was kindly, that she had known suffering . . for years of depression leave their mark when a mother has six children to bring up.

In the last few years Mrs Gibson lived alone in a miner's cottage. And surely no one had better earned the right to take her ease and enjoy the respect of others.

Yet there was never a time her young minister, Mr Nesham, came to see her that she did not rise to her feet as a mark of respect. It meant putting out a steadying hand to the edge of the table beside her rocking-chair and pulling herself laboriously to her feet, but she did it.

At first the young man was embarrassed and he protested, but all her life Mrs Gibson had stood when a man of God had entered her home, and to the end she would not change.

So different from many visits a minister pays nowadays, where young folk sit around as though he wasn't even there.

Maybe we're old-fashioned, but I can't help thinking with Mr Nesham that as the old folk leave us, so also does a little grace. . . . .

WEDNESDAY—APRIL 11.

THE stars like jewels shine at night,
  The Alps are crowned with snow ;
How wonderful a springtime wood,
  A field where daisies grow !
But to the housewife, bless her heart,
  There's nothing quite so fine
As sun-warmed, wind-blown washing that's
  A-drying on the line !

THE FRIENDSHIP BOOK

THE Lady of the House has one fault : She just won't do one thing at a time.

I mean that she refuses to change her library book at the public library, returning her own book only. She must pop round to Mrs Dun's and pick up her library book because Mrs Dun is looking after her invalid father ; and she must take back Mrs Strang's book because Mrs Strang can't get out . . . and when she calls with new library books for these neighbours she takes them a few sweets. . . .

I try to get her out of this bad habit, but it's no use !

I DOUBT if anyone outside Aberdeen ever heard of Janet Melville—yet all over the world many, many people should bless her name.

Miss Melville was a quiet, humble soul, and the most important thing in her life was her Sunday school class at St Nicholas Church.

Just picture her, a little grey-haired figure, with a group of spellbound boys round her. . . . Listen, quietly, as she tells them the stories of the men and women who carry the Word into far countries.

And what an amazing outcome it all had. No fewer than five of the boys became great missionaries.

There was Alexander Shepherd, of Rajputana ; James Webster, of Manchuria ; Andrew Cruickshank, of Calabar, friend and co-worker of Mary Slessor ; James Shepherd, of Udaipur ; and Robert Laws, of Livingstonia.

Why, when Miss Melville knew that Robert Laws wanted to be a missionary she even saw to it that his fees were paid from her own savings.

I sometimes think we little know what mighty works are being wrought in quiet places.

THE LEGIONS OF SPRING

The tulip army's on parade,
  Their banners deck the land;
In orange, gold and red arrayed,
  Like grenadiers they stand,
Awaiting word to march and bring
  To town the tidings of the spring.

DAVID HOPE

THE OPTIMIST

Whoever would have thought it!
A blackbird in the yard!
Building 'mid the engines
In happy disregard.
Never doubting she would find
The hearts of men were warm and kind.

DAVID HOPE

SATURDAY—APRIL 14.

I NEVER cease to wonder at the miracle of the human spirit.

Take this, for instance, from John Laffin's splendid book " Digger," the story of the Australian soldier.

A Queenslander, who lay waiting quietly for stretcher-bearers, had been severely wounded in the ribs, chest and throat.

" Does it hurt?" he was asked.

" Heck, no !" croaked the Digger. " Only when I laugh."

SUNDAY—APRIL 15.

AND the multitudes that went before Him, and that followed, cried, saying, Hosanna to the Son of David : Blessed is He that cometh in the name of the Lord ; Hosanna in the highest.

MONDAY—APRIL 16.

WHAT does your faith mean to you?

As the Rev. Thomas Jarvie put it, we can say, " I believe in God, so what?" Or we can say, " I believe in God, therefore . . ."

The first way is by far the easier. It's easy to go to church on Sunday, to the Guild or Men's Club, to drop our offering in the plate—and think that's the end of our obligations.

On the other hand, we can believe in God, therefore . . . *therefore* we go out of our way to help the old body down the road who can't get out on icy streets. *Therefore* we go to cheer up a neighbour in hospital who hasn't been too well. *Therefore* we try to live up to all the demands which faith imposes.

The reward is an inner peace and a strengthening of the character that an easy faith will never give.

TUESDAY—APRIL 17.

IF you waited outside Mayfield House, Edinburgh, any Sunday morning just before eleven you'd notice visitors going in through the gates . . . and, shortly afterwards, out they come again, each pushing a wheel-chair with someone in it.

Mayfield House is a Cheshire Foundation Home for folk who can't get around by themselves any more. And there was no way of getting them to the church, except by pushing them.

So what do you think? Members of St Serf's Church nearby volunteered to push the handicapped folk in their chairs down to the kirk and push them back again after the service. Why, on Sunday there are as many as ten wheel-chairs in merry procession!

Indeed, the folk from Mayfield have become so much part of the congregation that two rows of seats have been specially removed in church so that the wheel-chairs can be lined up in a row for the service.

Of course, when you're confined to a chair, you can't stand up to sing—but these brave folk manage jolly well sitting down. And when the service is over, there are willing hands to push out the chairs and wheel them back to Mayfield again.

Here's Francis Gay saluting the friendly neighbours of East Trinity Road.

WEDNESDAY—APRIL 18.

MINE the clouds so white and high,
Mine a continent of sky ;
Mine the blossom on the tree—
And the birds which sing for me.
Mine the garden—soil and sod—
Glowing at a touch from God.
From my window by the sink
I see more than you might think !

THURSDAY—APRIL 19.

A MAN stands in the garden of a country cottage. The garden is tidy, and the lawn is as smooth as a piece of green velvet. The white-washed walls of the house sparkle like snow.

For this man and his wife it was a dream almost come true. He was retiring soon, and the house was to be their new home. They'd saved carefully for it— a place in the country with a garden at the front for flowers, and a bit at the back for hens and vegetables.

For six months they had worked away, getting the place into fine order, and now they were waiting for the furniture to be moved in.

Then suddenly the man was called home from work. His wife had died suddenly. She had come home from shopping, sat down in a chair . . . and passed away.

How cruel life can be. All the planning and dreams that the couple had shared have been shattered in one blow, and now a lonely old man, visiting the cottage for the last time, can only think sadly of all that might have been. . . .

FRIDAY—APRIL 20.

ANNIE WILL is 81 and lives four storeys up in a tenement.

It's a grey building in a grey street, but I doubt if anyone will ever know just how much sunshine has been shed from Annie's little home.

" What does God give me money for if it's not to do good, Francis?" she once said to me when I called on her. " It would be dreadful to arrive at the Golden Gates with £2 in my hand and have St Peter say, ' What are you doing with that? Get away back with it !' "

What a happy way to look on money !

SATURDAY—APRIL 21.

SOME of us are fighting our battles without God. It is fine, but it is foolish. Lift up your hearts ! Let God come in like sunshine into a dark room.

Pray before you begin your tasks ; and you will find that strength and comfort are yours, sufficient for all your needs, and that you will win through to peace at the end of the day—not by raining proud blows against Fate, but by humbly walking with God.

SUNDAY—APRIL 22.

AND as they were eating, Jesus took bread, and blessed, and brake it ; and He gave to the disciples, and said, Take, eat ; this is My body. And He took a cup, and gave thanks, and gave to them, saying, Drink ye all of it ; For this is My blood of the covenant, which is shed for many unto remission of sins.

MONDAY—APRIL 23.

FRIEND, Easter has two messages for us.

First—It reminds us that life triumphs over death. Second—It is never too late to start again.

This is a challenge to you and me. Let us take a keen look at ourselves. Seeing ourselves as we really are is not a pleasant business—especially if we compare what we are with what we once hoped to be.

And all this perhaps prompts us to feel it's just no use . . . we'll never be any better.

This is just where Easter comes crashing into our lives, with the startling revelation that we have only to go down on our knees and ask God to forgive us and to make us anew. . . . No matter what a poor thing we have made of the years that are past, this Easter Day can be for us the beginning of a new life.

TUESDAY—APRIL 24.

YEARS ago, when the Rev. James Mitchell was a student, he was sent up to the parish of Kilmorack, near Beauly.

The minister, Dr Rankine, was retiring after spending almost the whole of his life there in the big, rambling manse on the road to Glen Affric. He had preached from the nearby kirk, reared his family there, grown old there. Now the time had come for him to leave the church and the friendly house.

The rooms were empty, and the windows uncurtained, as Dr Rankine and his wife passed through the door for the last time. Sadly the old minister turned the key on his past life. . . .

Then he and his wife did a lovely thing. Together they knelt down on the doorstep with clasped hands, and Dr Rankine offered a prayer—a prayer of thanks for their old home; for its shelter and kindness over the years; for the happiness, aye, and the sadness, too, that its walls had known, and for the love that had never been wanting within.

In a moment or two the old couple were on their feet again, and with one last look they left the old house. Yet the spirit of their benediction remained.

WEDNESDAY—APRIL 25.

NOW, hurry, hurry, postman,
        Don't linger on the stairs;
Don't chatter with the neighbours
        About their joys or cares,
For Granny, who is lonely,
        Is watching out for you.
Suppose her boy's not written,
        Whatever will she do?
Hurry, postman, up the stairs—
God has answered Granny's prayers!

THURSDAY—APRIL 26.

AT the old people's flats there's a green circle with five fine trees in it. Not long ago, however, some boys started slashing the trees.

That was more than Mrs Tannahill could stand. She collared the biggest boy, and said :

" Listen, you ! When you've finished spoiling these trees and you go home, remember your door is made of wood ; so is the chair you'll sit on and the table you eat at. If ever you see a cross or a crucifix, remember that Christ was nailed to a wooden cross. And let me tell you this—you'll die one day and be buried in a wooden coffin . . . and where's all the wood to come from if we destroy trees before their time, eh?"

Whether it was what Mrs Tannahill said or the intense way she said it I do not know. All I know is that the young hooligans went off, leaving the five trees to grow in peace.

FRIDAY—APRIL 27.

AT the end of a long and tiring day, Mum was gathering up toys left lying around on the living-room floor—gathering them up and putting them in a cupboard, and wishing. . . .

Oh, wishing there were no toys to gather up or bits of paper with scribbles on them or books needing to be shut . . . wishing, for that matter there were no bothersome, harassing, noisy, demanding children to wear her to a shadow.

Then came the thought : What would it be like to have no children to love, and no love from any little folk?

And the thought was so frightening that although she'd meant to scold, she went into the bedroom and kissed all three !

SATURDAY—APRIL 28.

THE worst has happened. . . .

Perhaps tragedy has overwhelmed you, your heart is broken, your hopes and dreams are gone. . . . This is the end. Or so it may seem to you.

Let me say this to you—This is *not* the end.

Somehow, when we fall in the dark, and after what seems endless misery, we at last begin to see a faint light . . . slowly life takes on a new interest and challenge . . . we have something to live for.

Which means that this is *not* the end, but a new beginning.

SUNDAY—APRIL 29.

AND if thy brother sin against thee, go, shew him his fault between thee and him alone : if he hear thee, thou hast gained thy brother.

MONDAY—APRIL 30.

A LITTLE service is being conducted in a common lodging-house where gather men, many of whom have lost their jobs, money, friends, hopes.

Suddenly the mission chaplain—Mr John H. Trotter—raises his voice and says imperatively—" You men playing cards there—listen a moment to me !"

Down go the cards.

" Men," says Mr Trotter, " each of you had a mother. Suppose she could see you *now* . . ."

" God forbid," calls one down-and-out.

And then in the silence a dozen men are wiping tears from their eyes with rough, grimy hands. It is temporary maudlin sentiment, to be sure, and very soon they'll be back to their old ways again . . .

But once, long ago, they were bright laddies who could say their prayers. How did the rot set in?

MAY

THE sun shone warm and bright when I visited a large colliery recently.

On the surface, the great colliery was quiet and almost deserted.

Suddenly a phone bell rang . . . there had been an accident and an injured miner was coming up the pit . . . his ribs had been crushed.

When I saw him brought into the sunlight, his young face was grey with shock and pain under its coating of black dust. The blackened faces of his four mates who carried the stretcher were grim with anxiety. Had they been quick enough. . . .?

Quick? They had rescued their young friend, given him aid, gently wrapped him in blankers, brought him almost a mile underground—at one point along a seam only 26 inches high—and here they were on the surface to meet the ambulance within half an hour of the accident.

And all the time I had basked in the sun hundreds of feet above them, in a world unaware.

I couldn't help thinking what a parable this was of life itself—how in our darkest moments we are often nearer the light than we realise.

WEDNESDAY—MAY 2.

HOW lucky is that man, though poor,
Though trouble is his lot,
Though half a hundred joys he lacks,
And genius he is not . . .
If, when his job is done, he knows
There's something good in life :
A home where he'll be welcomed by
A sweet and loving wife.

THE LITTLE ROADS

Oh, some are for the highway
That roars from town to town,
But I am for the narrow way
That wanders up and down,
By stream and hill and lochan's breast
To reach the Islands of the Blest.

DAVID HOPE

LOST !

Lost your daddy on the beach?
Don't worry any more.
We'll find him for you in a jiff—
That's what police are for.

So dry your eyes, young feller.
  Show the man you are.
You can tell your pals tomorrow
  You were in the radio car.

DAVID HOPE

THE DAY'S WORK

The liner, she's a lady,
  The tug no thing of beauty,
But the tug it comes in handy
  For a humdrum sort of duty.
Thus the Lord Almighty planned it
  Since the world was first begun,
Be you big or be you little,
  There's a job for everyone.

DAVID HOPE

THURSDAY—MAY 3.

I WONDER if you'd like to hear how young Brian Reid lost his job?

Brian is a schoolboy. His job was to blow the pipe organ in the village church on Sunday mornings.

The minister, Dr Millar, told the congregation the kirk hadn't been decorated for many years.

He wrote a letter to every one of the 260 members, and asked them if they'd give something to help the fund. He said he would sit in the manse on a certain day and receive their offerings with thanks.

I don't know what Dr Millar expected. But, believe it or not, by the time the manse door was closed that night, nearly £1000 had been given in sums from as much as £100 down to pennies from the children.

So, wonderful to relate, the church was not only redecorated, but new electric lighting and heating was installed—and an electric blower for the organ !

A wonderful effort, you'll agree—even if it did cost young Brian his job !

FRIDAY—MAY 4.

HEARD the true story of the American Congressman, Sol Bloom?

He was something of a character—and he knew a good deal about life. Sure as the sun came up, Sol walked to his office, thinking thoughts about Sol Bloom . . . not forgetting a few about other people.

And he had one curious habit—he always dropped a coin on the pavement.

"Say," inquired a friend "what's the idea?"

Sol grinned, "Somebody's sure to find it," he replied. "And they'll be happy all day !"

Nice to go through life making people happy . . . even if you don't know the people and never see them smiling.

SATURDAY—MAY 5.

A FRIEND came across these words in his reading the other day. He says they have challenged him and perhaps they may challenge others :—

"He has achieved success who has lived well, laughed often and loved much ; who has gained the respect of intelligent men and the love of little children; who has always looked for the best in others and given the best he had—in other words, one who has left the world a little better than he found it."

SUNDAY—MAY 6.

A SOFT answer turneth away wrath : but a grievous word stirreth up anger.

MONDAY—MAY 7.

I SAT on a sunny stone wall and watched the swallows. The thought occurred to me that the last time I had sat on that wall there had not been a swallow in sight. That had been on a sunny afternoon in February. No swallows then. Lots of them now. Where had they come from? And how had they found their way over thousands of miles of land and sea, probably flying much of the time by night?

It was comfortable sitting there on the sun-drenched wall . . . waiting for the Lady of the House to come across the field. Maybe I was wasting time. I do not think my idle speculation got me very far . . . but this is a wonderful and a mysterious world, isn't it? Ought we not, now and then, to think about the miracles which are part and parcel of our surroundings and of our lives?

So there I sat—and kept on sitting, watching the swallows, and wondering.

I have a feeling that I could have done worse.

TUESDAY—MAY 8.

I CANNOT blame people for being depressed—I am sometimes depressed myself. But if—as sometimes happens—people I meet are wallowing in depression and making themselves and everybody else miserable by gathering up armfuls of everything that's wrong in this old world, I feel like remarking as Jay Franklin once did—" The times are not so bad as they seem . . . they couldn't be !"

WEDNESDAY—MAY 9.

NOW if by chance you want a thrill,
But don't know how to find it,
Why not take someone by surprise—
Let flowers sweetly say it?
The thrill you give will thrill you, too—
I hope that you will try it !

THURSDAY—MAY 10.

THE long evenings are with us . . . watch out ! And what's the meaning of that warning?

Well, your old friend Francis Gay doesn't want to go down in history as the world's most melancholy fellow, but he does want to say this : It will soon be October, and once it's October it will be November in five minutes, November with chilly winds and fogs and dark days and darker nights . . . gardens bereft of beauty and country lanes too muddy to walk in.

Nice cheery sort of chap, Francis Gay, isn't he?

But you see, folks, the long, light evenings are with us . . . and before you and I have time to turn round, believe me the long light evenings will have come and gone, and you'll have missed those country walks and those pleasant little chats over the fence.

The long, light evenings are with us. Enjoy them !

FRIDAY—MAY 11.

FOR a long time Alex. Cussons wanted to give his wife a very special gift . . . a damask rose.

He knew exactly the scent he wanted. He remembered it from the time he first saw the beautiful rose that was even older than the Holy Land from whence it came.

For years Alex. searched rose-gardens in England and on the Continent. He tried hundreds of thousands of blooms, but always the scent he sought eluded him. Yet, there was always a chance if he kept on.

Sure enough, one day in Chilwell, Nottingham, he was walking through a rose-garden where the roses didn't yet have names. He cupped one rose in his hand, sniffed—and he had found it.

Mrs Cussons now has the rose growing at their home and the grower has named it after her.

Of course, she's thrilled. So is Alex. And so was I when I heard that the rose, Wendy Cussons, had won a gold medal in an international show in Holland.

SATURDAY—MAY 12.

WHEN he returned home from school, young Andrew's mother asked, " Well, Andy, did you like the two pieces of cake I gave you for lunch?"

Andrew went very red. " Well," he explained slowly, " you see, David Davidson had forgotten his lunch, so I had to give him mine."

" Oh? And why had you to give him yours?"

" Well, he felt terrible hungry, you see ; and he hasn't a father, and I have . . . and if anything happened to David where would his mother be?"

I am glad that Andy did not get into trouble. He might, of course, have shared his lunch with David . . . but love never does things by halves.

Maybe this old world wouldn't be too bad if more of us took a hint from wee Andy?

SUNDAY—MAY 13.

AND while they abode in Galilee, Jesus said unto them, The Son of man shall be delivered up into the hands of men ; and they shall kill Him, and the third day He shall be raised up.

MONDAY—MAY 14.

WHAT'S wrong with the world?

How is it that some folk have everything and others nothing? Why are we piling up guided missiles? Why do such a large number of people get killed on the roads? How is it that in an age of plenty, people "couldn't care less," take their own lives, prefer living by violence to going straight?

Ask the politicians, economists, doctors, and you'll get a different answer every time.

But on his 80th birthday Bertrand Russell told us what it was. He said—" The root of the matter is a very simple, old-fashioned thing . . . the thing I mean—please forgive me for mentioning it—is love, Christian love." He added—" If you love, you have a motive for existence, a reason for courage, an imperative necessity for intellectual honesty."

Christ himself said it long before Bertrand Russell—" Love God—and your neighbour as yourself."

TUESDAY—MAY 15.

MORE than 40 years ago, during the 1914-18 war, Archie Black went on leave to Cairo.

He stayed in the Anzac Hostel, and the first thing he noticed when he opened the main door was a huge printed notice which read :—

Be the man your mother thinks you are.

The words made such an impact on Mr Black that he never forgot them and I doubt if he ever will.

WEDNESDAY—MAY 16.

IF you can mend a broken heart,
   Now full of care—run, mend it !
If you can lend a helping hand
   Sometime, somewhere, please lend it.
If you've a worthwhile job to do,
   Scorn all delay, and do it,
For those who might have served but failed
   Will come one day to rue it.

THURSDAY—MAY 17.

NOT long ago the Rev. John Birkbeck, of Aberdeen, returned home after working for three months in West Africa. While he was there he visited Calabar, where Mary Slessor, the Dundee mill-girl, carried out her great missionary work.

When Mr Birkbeck spoke at a meeting there, he mentioned that he came from Aberdeen, where Mary Slessor was born in 1848, and that he knew Wishart Church, Dundee—the very kirk that helped to influence Mary to become a missionary.

At this an old man rose to his feet, his arms outstretched and his eyes shining with excitement and happiness. It turned out that the man, now over 90 years old, had been one of the first Mary Slessor had won to the Christian faith when she went to Calabar !

The old man was just a boy of nine or ten when he first saw " the great mother." Yet he had never forgotten her, and the faith she had passed on to him had been his most precious possession.

Mr Birkbeck told me the Africans he met read the Bible with a Scottish accent, just as Mary Slessor had read it to their fathers and grandfathers.

Surely this story shows the limitless achievement of a girl who had a faith that is shining still.

FRIDAY—MAY 18.

WE cannot tell when that day will be, but come it must—the day when for you and me the sands of time are running out.

Will there be any joy in our hearts then?

I think, perhaps, we will assess life anew, and realise that it isn't who we are that matters so very much, but what we are. It's not the money we've made, but how we've made it. It's not what we've got, but what we've given away.

It's not the big things we've done that will count, but all the little kindnesses and unremembered words of cheer or praise or encouragement.

It isn't the urgent importance of getting things done which means anything towards the end—it's having time to be gracious, for turning aside and looking at the good world, giving our Maker a chance to fill our hearts with wonder, love and praise.

SATURDAY—MAY 19.

IT may come as a surprise to some that two years ago the Selection Panel of the Church of Scotland did something it hasn't done for ten years. At one sitting it interviewed 23 applicants for the ministry.

In other words, more men are wanting to preach than most of us ever imagined—and these applicants are older men and men of ability and experience.

Quite a few have deliberately turned aside from jobs with far better prospects and incomes than they can ever hope to secure as preachers.

Could it be that at this very time when religion seems to be in eclipse great souls and deep thinkers are becoming aware, as never before, that if the human race is to survive and if tomorrow is to hold anything worthwhile, the millions must be brought back to worship and to a new conception of brotherly love?

SUNDAY—MAY 20.

FOR mine eyes are unto Thee, O God the Lord: in Thee do I put my trust; leave not my soul destitute.

MONDAY—MAY 21.

SOME time ago the statisticians of Wisconsin University were worried. So they decided to inquire into the sort of things people worry about.

They found that 40 per cent. of our worries are about things which never happen.

They found also that 30 per cent. of the things most of us worry about are things which have happened, and which therefore no amount of worrying now will be able to alter.

Third, they discovered that 22 per cent. of our worries are needless. So you don't need to be very good at figures to see that 92 out of every 100 worries are things there's just no point in worrying about!

TUESDAY—MAY 22.

A GIRL was ill and she received a card from the woman who helped to clean in the house.

It was a normal get-well card, but under the signature were the four letters R.S.A.C.

The girl tried to puzzle out what they meant. So did the whole family, but it remained a mystery.

Finally they asked the woman. Her reply was a delightful surprise, for the letters simply mean—" Remember, someone always cares."

She said she always put the letters on cards to people who were ill or distressed, simply because—someone always does care.

Four little letters. You might like to use them, too, some time!

IN PRAISE OF DUCKS

The throstle's song to charm us,
The night owl to alarm us.
When ducks parade
They mock the staid
*   And with good humour arm us!*

DAVID HOPE

TAKE YOUR TIME

A one-horse road, a one-horse speed,
Far from the busy ways.
Oh, what can beat a one-horse road
In apple-blossom days!

DAVID HOPE

WEDNESDAY—MAY 23.

IF nobody smiled and nobody cheered,
 And nobody helped us along,
If each every minute looked after himself,
 And good things all went to the strong ;
If nobody cared just a little for you
 And nobody thought about me,
And each stood alone in the battle of life,
 What a dreary old world this would be !

THURSDAY—MAY 24.

AN old minister who had laboured for over 40 years in a poor parish in New York felt within himself he had achieved little or nothing.

In his despair he wrote to Bishop Whipple of Minnesota, a brilliant churchman of his day.

The Bishop hastened to New York and soon he was listening to the troubles of the old preacher. " I've toiled and prayed for 40 years," he said. " But what have I achieved? Look at yourself, Bishop—you are successful. Why am I a failure?"

The Bishop turned to the minister. " Do you remember Mary?" he asked. " She used to attend your communicants' class many years ago. She had to leave New York to look after her brother . . ."

Bishop Whipple added that the brother had been a no-good and in one of his more sober moments had asked the sister why she bothered with him.

" Because of my faith," Mary had said. The brother sneered—" Your faith . . . what's faith?" The girl handed him the notes the old minister had given her at the communicants' class. " Read these," she told him. " They will tell you what faith is."

The Bishop paused in his story and looked at the old man. " Sir," he said quietly, " that drunken brother is the man who is speaking to you now . . ."

FRIDAY—MAY 25.

NOT long ago Major Goodsell, a Salvation Army officer, visited an old woman who was lonely and downhearted.

Miss Goodsell found her with tears in her eyes. She'd been out doing her shopping and had lost a pound note. And when you've only a pension, a pound is an awful lot of money.

Major Goodsell promised to do what she could and went back to her headquarters. She had scarcely sat down when there came a knock at the door. It was a little girl with a basket. Her mother had been doing the shopping and had decided to buy a little extra and send it along to the Salvation Army!

Need I tell you what Major Goodsell did next? She went right back to the old woman and handed over the groceries.

And you needn't tell that old soul—or Major Goodsell—that it was all only coincidence . . .

SATURDAY—MAY 26.

IT beats me," said our young neighbour to the Lady of the House.

" It's always the same," she went on breathlessly. " Never a day long enough to get done half the things I have to do . . . Yet my granny had six children, and I've only two. She was poor, and my hubby's doing well. She never had any domestic help. She never had a vacuum cleaner   yet the house was spotless, and everybody's clothes were neat and clean and beautifully ironed.

" And that isn't all ! She seemed to have bags of time to spare !

" Yet here am I, with every labour-saving gadget, a bubble-car of my own, a modern house . . . and I'm rushed off my feet every day . . It beats me !"

SUNDAY—MAY 27.

TEACH me to do Thy will; for Thou art my God:
Thy spirit is good; lead me in the land of up-
rightness.

MONDAY—MAY 28.

I TOOK a stroll in the quiet evening—birds singing
everywhere in the lane not far from my door;
and as I wandered back I met two young folk, arms
round each other, strolling happily in wonderland.

There came to mind four lines perhaps forgotten
now—four lines by Robert Tannahill, a Paisley
weaver, who died at 36 after writing much sweet and
tender poetry. He never married, and yet . . . who
knows what dreams he had in springtime, for we
owe to him the song with the verse:

When gloamin' treads the heels o' day,
And birds sit courtin' on the spray,
Along the flow'ry hedge I stray
To meet mine ain dear somebody!

TUESDAY—MAY 29.

SHEILA was only two and a half years old and
going to church was still a new and exciting
experience for her.

The first part of the service went off with Sheila
behaving like a little lady. Then came a prayer
and the slight hush before the next hymn.

Suddenly up piped Sheila. "Everybody stand up,
sing!" she said, her little voice sounding clearly
through the church.

Everybody did stand up—and how they sang!

Good for you, Sheila. You certainly have the right
idea, for I always feel that praise has a better chance
of reaching heaven if it has zest and joy in it.

WEDNESDAY—MAY 30.

HOW beautiful, how wonderful,
If for a little bit
I'd nothing all day long to do
But sit and sit and sit !
No chores at all, no pots to wash. . . .
And yet I wonder if
A week of such rare luxury
Would simply bore me stiff !

THURSDAY—MAY 31.

THIS, in a way, is the story of an old kitchen table. It stood in a hut in an internment camp in France over 40 years ago. It was to this camp that Dr Albert Schweitzer, the great missionary and organist, was taken when he was interned as an " enemy alien " of the French Empire during the first world war.

They couldn't make an exception of him, missionary though he was, so they brought him all the way from Africa, where he was striving to build a hospital to care for the sick and dying among native tribes.

One day his gaze fell upon the old kitchen table that stood in the corner. He drew a chair up to it. Then, placing his hands on the edge of the table, as if it were a keyboard, he began to play.

Of course, no sound came. But in his mind, Dr Schweitzer heard wondrous music. Day after day he " practised," and when at last he was released he found to his joy that the magic had not left his fingers.

Almost straight away he gave concerts to raise money for the rebuilding of his hospital in Africa, and such was the beauty of his playing that thousands all over the world clamoured to hear him. And to think that kitchen table helped to make this possible.

JUNE

EVERYBODY hits a bad patch sooner or later.
But some folk come to the point when they are
quite sure they simply cannot keep on any longer,
convinced that no one else has ever had such a bitter
experience or such a piling up of one misfortune upon
another. " This is the end," they say.

Everybody—except the coward—battles on, and
wins through to days which are brighter and kinder
than they ever thought possible.

Everybody finds that when their own strength is
insufficient they can, by earnest prayer, tap a new
supply of spiritual power. We win our greatest fights
against despair, not on our feet, but on our knees.

I REMEMBER it every time the second of June
comes round.

A girl asked us all to pray for her on that day.
Her voice went into millions of homes and touched
millions of hearts, for the girl was our Queen, and
the second of June was her Coronation Day.

" I want to ask you all," she said, " whatever
your religion may be, to pray for me—to pray that
God may give me wisdom and strength to carry out
the solemn promises I shall be making, and that I
may faithfully serve Him and you, all the days of
my life. . . ."

The glitter and pomp of the great day have faded,
but one thing can never fade—the Queen's example
of her faith in the power of prayer.

That is why, every second of June, I give thanks
that we are blessed with such a gracious and God-
fearing woman as our Queen.

SUNDAY—JUNE 3.

AND God blessed the seventh day, and hallowed it : because that in it He rested from all His work which God had created and made.

MONDAY—JUNE 4.

WHAT a wealthy man old Diogenes must have been !

He lived about 400 years before Christ . . . and was so poor, they say, that his house was a tub. Nothing more. No rates or taxes. Mighty clever was he, for he managed to live—and to enjoy living.

One day Alexander the Great paid the old Greek a visit. He said to Diogenes, " Is there anything I can do for you?"

" Yes," replied the poor rich man, " move a step to one side, please, so that I can see the sun !"

TUESDAY—JUNE 5.

YOU and I do seem to get a lot of what we don't like, don't we?

Maybe it's one illness after another, or ill-luck seems to dog us. Funny, isn't it, but if there's a nasty job to do at the office or shop or factory, it somehow seems to fall to you, doesn't it?

Yes, you haven't to be very old before you realise that life's unfair.

There are two things you can do about it. You can rebel against it and get angry and cynical and bitter, all of which only makes matters worse.

Or you can keep cracking on with a grin and a bit of humour, somehow rising above all the ills of life, and thereby having the admiration and respect of folk who know you, and—of course, as you'll agree— enjoying life immensely, however unkind it is.

WEDNESDAY—JUNE 6.

*K*NOCK *at the door, face with a grin,*
  Neighbour who asks, " May I come in?"
Oh, what a thrill in a long day.
Just a wee chat—up and away.
Living alone—two flights of stairs ;
Nice to have proof somebody cares !

THURSDAY—JUNE 7.

I RAISE my hat to Jim's Mum.

I met the two of them out together one Saturday afternoon—Mum looking wonderfully young and bright. I ventured to tell her I liked her wee hat, and she ticked me off for doing so, but treated me to a lovely smile.

Jim said nothing, though. Jim never does. Poor Jim never does anything, except sit in his wheeled chair, his head on one side, his eyes staring into space.

For sixteen years Mum has cared for Jim—done everything for him ; fed him, dressed him, taken him in his chair, denied herself for him . . and never a word of thanks, never a smile or a pat of the hand.

Of all thankless jobs, hers seems the most thankless. Of all hard jobs, hers seems the hardest—and it is harder than ever when she sees teenage boys and girls running or shouting or laughing.

Couldn't Jim be in some home?

Of course he could, but Mum feels she wants to look after him herself, to do her utmost to make his life as comfortable as she can, to spare him any dread or any loneliness. I don't say whether she is right or wrong . . . I merely state that this gallant little body counts no sacrifice too great.

May God continue to give her the strength she needs.

FRIDAY—JUNE 8.

GEORGE CASSELLS died as he lived, working for the cause he believed in with all his heart.

He was an architect. As a student, he rose at six in the morning to study, and all his life he retained the habit. It was in these early hours that George found he could best serve the Church he loved.

He drew up plans for new churches, for repairs and restorations, and the more he did, the more work came in. After 30 years it told on his health, but he kept going on.

I know he didn't profit one penny from all his industry for the Church. He had to accept his architect's fees, but for 30 years he always found a way to pay every penny back into the Church and its work.

These are days of get-rich-quick, but George Cassells was rich in the real things of life when he passed on.

SATURDAY—JUNE 9.

ONE of the saddest things in life is coming up against people who are short of money

Some folk haven't enough to live on in reasonable comfort—it just happens so, as a result of no end of things. They are not at all to blame.

But so many folk have gone out of their way to make trouble for themselves—they just won't put by for a rainy day.

The least bit of thrift, the smallest of sacrifices, would have enabled them to bypass trouble.

It's difficult to be sorry for a man who can't get his shoes mended because he's drunk every penny !

What has all this to do with you? Nothing, I hope. But if by chance there is not a fortune coming into your house week by week, remember that folk who save for rainy days never get any rainy days !

SUNDAY—JUNE 10.

THEREFORE thou shalt love the Lord thy God, and keep His charge, and His statutes, and His judgments, and His commandments, alway.

MONDAY—JUNE 11.

IT all started when the Rev. J. Trainer, chaplain of a naval barracks in Sydney, was planning the altar in the new chapel there. He wanted it to be a rather special altar—so he wrote to over 100 churches in all parts of the world asking if he might have a stone from each, to be included in the altar.

Mr Trainer realised that men of many lands would pass through the barracks in Sydney, and he felt it would be a link with home for these men if the altar contained even the tiniest piece of their homeland.

And what a heart-warming response he had.

Stones arrived from all over the world. There's a slab from Zanzibar Cathedral, and others from Calcutta, Singapore and Jerusalem Cathedral.

There are stones from the great cathedrals of England, a piece of Peterhead granite from St Machar's Cathedral in Aberdeen, and six stone slabs from the crypt of Glasgow Cathedral.

The new chapel is a witness to the countless centuries of faith in many lands.

TUESDAY—JUNE 12.

I LIKE this little story. One day a three-year-old boy had been chastised for being naughty. When bedtime came he said his prayers, praying for everyone he knew—except his mother.

When he rose from his knees he turned to his mother and said · " I suppose you noticed YOU wasn't in it?"

WEDNESDAY—JUNE 13.

IF you've lost hope, and feel that life
Can never be worth while,
And that—however long the road—
You'll neither sing nor smile ,
Take courage, friend ; plod bravely on,
And scorn to curse or whine.
The day may dawn when once again
For you the sun will shine.

THURSDAY—JUNE 14.

IT was only by chance that I saw the few lines, tucked away in a page in my newspaper.

They told me that a man had passed away who, I believe, is worthy to rank with the greatest.

He was Dr George Simpson, and I doubt if one in ten thousand here has ever heard of him. Yet today countless men, women and children owe their very lives to him, for he was founder—with his friend, the Rev. John Flynn—of the great Australian Flying Doctor service.

At first it was just an idea, and Dr Simpson used to lie awake at night, planning that one day it might be more. He was saddened because in tiny homesteads at the back of beyond folk suffered and died because there was no doctor to go to them—and no way a doctor could reach them.

Then, in 1928, for the first time a doctor—George Simpson himself—took off on a flight of mercy, and since that day the Flying Doctors have become part of the very life of Australia. Planes can go in hours to places that would have taken weeks to reach otherwise. Lives are being saved, suffering eased, aye, and the dying comforted.

George Simpson is dead—but I am glad he did not die before he saw his dream come true.

FRIDAY—JUNE 15.

THIS is the story of an Irish minister whose church lay between Portrush and the Giant's Causeway. Every Sunday the preacher spoke of the wonder and the sacredness of the Sabbath.

But there came a Sunday when a tram service began to run past the church, taking tourists to and from the Giant's Causeway.

The old minister was shocked. The next Sunday he preached a spirited sermon on the meaning of the Sabbath and of the Commandment, " Remember the Sabbath Day to keep it holy."

As he was praying, one of the trams came rattling past the church.

The old minister broke off in the middle of his prayer, raised his eyes to Heaven, and cried out—

" Listen, Lord. You can hear it for yerself. It's comin' round the corner now !'

SATURDAY—JUNE 16.

IF you are utterly broken because of some bereavement, you may say Francis Gay doesn't know what he's talking about ; and you may add, " Now, if only he'd suffered a loss like mine. . . ."

What *can* tomorrow hold for you except the misery and loneliness of parting? Now that the loved one has gone, you *know* there can be no joy, and that nothing can ever again be worthwhile.

And yet the truth is that time does heal, if only partially. As time goes on there creeps here and there into your life some glimmer of light, some compensation for heartache.

Maybe you are sure this will never happen to you . . but, my friend, I have known deep sorrow, and have found that in time you learn to live with it and to find much that enriches and sweetens life.

SUNDAY—JUNE 17.

AND it came to pass, after three days they found Him in the temple, sitting in the midst of the doctors, both hearing them and asking them questions : And all that heard Him were amazed at His understanding and His answers.

MONDAY—JUNE 18.

I HAVE been asked many times for a definition of true courage—and I believe I have found one.

I cannot remember where I read it, and if any acknowledgment is due I pay it gladly in advance, for in these eight words the meaning of real Christian courage is perfectly summed up :—

" Courage is fear that has said its prayers."

TUESDAY—JUNE 19.

IF you ever visit Cidhmore, the Salvation Army's eventide home in Dundee, you will see a sermon on the mantelpiece in the hall. It reads :

" Some of us have to live with people whom we would not choose, who think in different ways from us, and hold opposing views. Who have annoying habits that are hard to tolerate, and stupid mannerisms that provoke and aggravate.

" But if we cannot change our home we must accept these things and shut our eyes to petty points that daily living brings. We must look out for virtues though the faults stand out much higher, for in every disposition there is something to admire.

" And, after all, if we could see the other person's point of view, we might think we were difficult and irritating too !"

It occurs to me this might apply just as well in your home and mine.

WEDNESDAY—JUNE 20.

How pleasant to be young and strong,
And dash around all day ;
How nice to have no end of pals
As young, and quite as gay !

How good, when youth and strength are gone,
Life's ashes growing cold,
To have one friend with whom to share
The joy of growing old !

THURSDAY—JUNE 21.

THE letter was addressed to a minister, and with it were two pounds and this note :—

" We are both in hospital, and although we can't do much, we'd like to do a little. Please use this to help some of the needy folk you meet, and tell them we'll be praying for them. From two who have been blessed."

The minister was so touched he tried to find the couple who sent the gift so that he could thank them.

And find them he did—in a hospital—a young man and his wife who had been there for years.

It seems they were stricken by the same illness and had to go to hospital together. Newspapers were almost their only contact with the outside world—and, as they read, they were saddened by how much tragedy and misery there was in the world outside.

For instance, when they read of a boy—motherless and unwanted—who was put on probation for stealing, they sent some money for him, and asked the minister to let the boy know they were thinking of him and praying for him.

In the same way they have sent gifts for others, although they themselves are not well-off.

What a marvellous spirit, isn't it?

FRIDAY—JUNE 22.

NOT, How did he die?
    But how did he live?
Not what did he gain?
But what did he give?
These are the units to measure the worth
Of a man as a man regardless of birth.
Not what was his station?
But had he a heart?
How did he play his God-given part?
Was he ever ready with a word of good cheer
To bring back a smile or to banish a tear?
Not what was his Church or what was his creed?
But had he befriended those really in need?
Not what did the words in the newspaper say?
But how many were sorry when he passed away?

SATURDAY—JUNE 23.

CONTRARY to local opinion, Mrs Fraser doesn't
    live alone.

If you'd asked me, I should most certainly have
told you that Mrs Fraser stayed by herself.

According to the Lady of the House, however, this
isn't so. There's Mrs Fraser's cat.

My wife was telling me about it the other day—
with a bit of mischief in her eyes, I think. You see,
it's dreadful coming in from your shopping and
having nobody to whom you can say you've met a
neighbour, nobody to whom you can remark that
the price of tomatoes is much too high !

But how lucky you are if, like Mrs Fraser, you
can climb up to your single room, unlock your door,
and (once you've got your breath) begin telling your
little friend all about everything ! Which (so the Lady
of the House assures me) is what Mrs Fraser does.

In that way loneliness is at least bearable.

SUNDAY—JUNE 24.

AND in the fourth watch of the night He came unto them, walking upon the sea.

MONDAY—JUNE 25.

ONE of the giants of our day has passed on—the Rev. Dr W. E. Sangster, preacher, inspiring writer, humorist and saint.

Here on my desk is a little note which his wife sent to all who had written to her in her sorrow—

" Mrs W. E. Sangster and her family thank you for your sympathy, and for all your love and prayers during her husband's long illness. Even in their grief they thank God for his example in their lives, for the ease of his passing and for his undimmed trust in the words he often quoted—

My knowledge of that life is small,
The eye of faith is dim ;
But 'tis enough the Christ knows all,
And I shall be with him.

" He is with Him now."

TUESDAY—JUNE 26.

DEAR Mr Gay,—

I am home now after our hollyday at Eastborne in a big hotel with a sea vue and waiters and Mum and Dad said it was expensive and nise and I liked it quite a bit, and it was funn on the shore but it was niser to get back and sea the puppie next door, and what I liked best was taiking some post cards to old Mrs Hunter and some bisskits, and she was so glad to sea me and I think evan a good holliday isn't as nise as doing things you like at home.

Yours with love,

Myra.

WEDNESDAY—JUNE 27.

GOT a little grievance?
  Feeling hurt, may be?
Think and think about it
  Till it's agony.
Lot of good it does you ;
  Makes you glum as glum.
Just look in your mirror—
  Watch the wrinkles come.
Shake yourself and do your stuff—
You've been wretched long enough !

THURSDAY—JUNE 28.

THE sun that filtered through the tall, stained-glass windows of the church shone brilliantly on over 100 nurses in their white starched caps and their crisp, neat uniforms. Each nurse wore her dark blue cloak and hood lined with scarlet.

What a splendid picture they made.

Why were all the nurses in church that morning? Because, over 100 years ago another dedicated nurse returned from the Crimean War, broken in health, but as strong and fearless in spirit as ever, and she set up the first proper scheme for training young nurses in their service to the sick and suffering.

Her name, of course, was Florence Nightingale— the Lady with the Lamp—and it was she who raised nursing from a level where hardly a woman would have considered it, to the selfless calling it is today.

The young nurses—and many of the folk they had nursed back to health—had gathered to honour Florence Nightingale's memory, to give thanks for the lives that have been saved in all these years, and to pray for the future.

Florence's lamp may have gone out long ago, but I know its light shines more brightly than ever.

THE FIRST TIME I —— !

You can speak of your tuna and shark
And other strange beasts of the dark.
But the biggest of thrills without doubt
Was the first time you landed a trout.
A whopper ! three ounces in weight.
Remember ? When you were just eight ?

DAVID HOPE

BOUNTY

See reflected in my bay
The glory of a summer day,
The image of the house and trees
Scarcely ruffled by a breeze ;
Bounteous nature giving twice
Lest one joy should not suffice.

DAVID HOPE

FRIDAY—JUNE 29.

ISN'T it strange that princes and kings and clowns that caper in sawdust rings, and common people, like you and me, are builders of Eternity? Each is given a bag of tools, a shapeless mass, a book of rules ; and each must make, ere life has flown, a stumbling block—or a stepping stone.

SATURDAY—JUNE 30.

THEY said he was the meanest man in London.

He lived and died over 200 years ago, and his name was Thomas Guy. His father was a coal-merchant, and Thomas himself became a bookseller. He dressed in threadbare clothes, and ate his dinner off his shop-counter with only an old newspaper for a tablecloth.

Not a likeable fellow at all—no love in his heart, or kindness in his hand, or so people said.

But how wrong they were. For in his lifetime Thomas Guy gave away thousands of pounds to folk he scarcely knew—to men whose businesses had crashed, to the poor, to young men starting off in life. And he warned them all to say nothing of it.

Not only that. It was he who built the hospital in London which now bears his name—Guy's Hospital, one of the foremost centres of healing and medicine in the world. Believe it or not, he gave more than a quarter of a million pounds to Guy's Hospital, and in doing so he gave to thousands a new chance of life. It may be that you owe thanks to Thomas Guy —for many discoveries have been made in his hospital, which revolutionised modern medicine.

So before we point the finger at the man next door, let us remember Thomas Guy, the so-called miser, and think again. For sometimes we little know what good our neighbour is doing by stealth.

JULY

I GLORIFIED Thee on the earth, having accomplished the work which Thou hast given Me to do.

YOU would never think of giving up your holiday for your kirk, would you?

Probably I wouldn't either. Yet the wonderful thing I discovered the other day is that no fewer than 1200 men and women did just that last year.

What's more, they were folk like you and me—husbands, wives, mothers, sons and daughters, from all sorts of jobs like shops, shipyards, mines, garages, busy hospitals, quiet lawyers' offices, railways, schools, and so on and on.

Oh, yes, there's hardly a job you could name that hasn't been represented at one time or another at St Ninian's Training Centre, Crieff, since it began its work. And the splendid thing is that all these workers come together to learn all they can about the one job they know in their hearts is the biggest of all. It is to spread the Word wherever it will be heard in their own neighbourhood.

One man at the centre was a former colonel who was training to be a minister. Another was a joiner who was going as a missionary-builder to Northern Rhodesia.

Some of those who gave up their holidays came straight from school. Another was a man of 87.

Yet, in their working together, each finds he has something to give the other as they learn to carry the kirk into corners it has never reached.

Each is enriched, and in the end I am sure they enrich many others.

TUESDAY—JULY 3.

NOTHING happened . . . that's why I'm writing about it.

Maybe that seems a bit queer to you. It's this way—The Lady of the House and I escaped for a day or two and went for a holiday on a farm.

One evening the Lady of the House sat in the big kitchen and helped our hostess to prepare vegetables for next day. So I took a stroll all by myself.

I lit a pipe. I walked into the evening sunshine—up the lane and into a silence that could be felt. . . .

The lane brought me to the little stone bridge over the burn, and there I stood. How long I stood I cannot say. Nobody talked to me. No surprising event took place. In fact, nothing happened.

But what an enriching experience that was . . . the quietness sinking into my soul ; the chance to do nothing and to let the fancy rove ; to listen to stillness, and ponder over past days and wonder about the days ahead . . . maybe to offer a wordless prayer for fresh courage and new strength. . . .

There was a star or two in the clear sky when I walked into the farm kitchen. The Lady of the House was laying the table for supper.

But neither then nor since has she ever asked what I did or where I went.

WEDNESDAY—JULY 4.

EASY to get depressed these days,
  Easy to feel afraid,
Easy to think the world's gone mad,
  Easy for dreams to fade.
But news we hear of things we fear
  Should never blind us to
The kindly, splendid, lovely things
  So many people do.

THURSDAY—JULY 5.

WHY do so many millions trek to the sea and the hills at this time of year?

Could it be the lure of big things? Do we go to the seaside partly because the sea is so wide and deep and permanent that it does us good to look at it?

Do we visit the wild Highlands because somehow, deep in the spirit, all the silly little vexations of life melt away as we look over the vast areas of wonder?

After all, you and I (as somebody once said) are but a little lower than the angels. It may sound absurd, but we are (or were meant to be) giants—immense men and women striding magnificently towards the stars . . . . and it's only because we neglect to pray and forget to worship that we shrivel into such miserable little anxious creatures.

FRIDAY—JULY 6.

A BELL was ringing above the roar of traffic in Glasgow. The time was 8.30 a.m.

I stepped out of the bustle of the busy thoroughfare—into the peace of St George's-Tron church.

There was soft organ music. The cross shone above the pulpit. In the pews were half a hundred folk—men and women, two schoolgirls, a coloured man. Two or three came late. One left early. Some were reading their Bibles. Several were praying.

Promptly at 8.35 the service began—a simple little service lasting only 15 minutes. We sang a hymn. There was a prayer, a Bible reading about Abraham, who went forth not knowing whither, a brief address, and the benediction.

This service, in the heart of Glasgow, takes place every morning of the week, except Saturday, and as I came away I couldn't help thinking what a wonderful way it is to start the day.

SATURDAY—JULY 7.

IN my reading I came across this wee bit of wisdom
passed on by Lord Baillieu.

Age is a quality of mind.
If you have left your dreams behind,
If hope is cold,
If you no longer plan ahead,
If your ambitions all are dead,
Then you *ARE* old.
But if of life you make the best,
And in your life you still have zest,
No matter how the birthdays fly,
No matter how the years go by,
You are *NOT* old.

SUNDAY—JULY 8.

HE that loveth Me not keepeth not My words.

MONDAY—JULY 9.

AS sure as I passed the house at the corner, John's
wife Mary would catch sight of me and give me
a wave, and I waved back.

How strange it is now to pass the house at the
corner *and not to wave to Mary*. Though well over
60, she always looked so young and kindly. She
went to sleep and never woke up. . . .

And if I miss Mary, what about John, her devoted
husband? They lived in retirement, went everywhere
together, stayed at home together.

But when John and I had a little chat the other
evening he wiped his eyes and made a gallant attempt
to smile. " I expect," said he, " the proper way to
look at it is this—not that she's gone away and left
me, but that she stayed with me for 40 years, and
made me happy all that time."

TUESDAY—JULY 10.

WHEN you don't know which way to turn, when every possible path seems fraught with danger or difficulty, when you are at your wits' end, and you find it impossible to make a wise decision, why not stop looking anxiously round and begin looking up?

Putting your troubles into God's hands, waiting for that quiet inward voice to direct your steps, trusting that things will work out in His time, His good time . . . this is the way to stride confidently out of the maze of bewilderment, knowing what to do and having the strength to do it.

WEDNESDAY—JULY 11.

YOU know you can't—you know, you know !
  You can't keep keeping on.
You can't believe or hope or dare ;
  Your faith and strength are gone.
You can't do this ; you can't do that—
  Useless to dream or plan . . .
And yet, if love be in your heart,
  You find somehow you CAN !

THURSDAY—JULY 12.

ALTHOUGH Sir Francis Bacon lived 450 years ago in a world very different from ours, he had things to say that you and I might well think about.

And he could say a mighty lot in a very few words. Take, for instance, the following and consider it :—

It is not what men eat but what they digest that makes them strong ; not what we gain but what we save that makes us rich ; not what we read but what we remember that makes us learned ; not what we preach but what we practise that makes us Christians.

FRIDAY—JULY 13.

A DETACHMENT of soldiers from the Gordon Highlanders and pipes and drums were attending a service in East St Nicholas Church, Aberdeen.

As the soldiers marched up King Street two wee laddies joined on behind them, as boys will. Right up to the corner they strode, right behind the last shining pair of boots. Round they wheeled into Union Street, past the watching crowds, and up to the gate of the churchyard. Nothing daunted, they followed the soldiers up the path, to the door.

There they faltered. They looked at each other—and whispered. Then they slipped away from the soldiers and went up to the beadle who stood by the step. "Hey, mister," piped up the spokesman. "How much is it to get in?"

Ay, it's a funny wee story—but isn't it sad that there are children today who, like these two, have never seen the inside of a church?

SATURDAY—JULY 14.

I WALKED two miles in the country with a blind man—an unforgettable experience.

We kept in step all the way, and the road was drenched with sunshine. The hedges seemed alive with singing birds. The sky was blue as blue. Everywhere there were flowers—and how green the grass, how magnificent the distant mountains.

And my companion missed it all!

As soon as I was home that night I went into my bedroom, closed the door, knelt by the bed and repeated, as a prayer, those words of John Keble's :—

Thou Who hast given me eyes to see
And love this sight so fair,
Give me a heart to find out Thee,
And read Thee everywhere.

SUNDAY—JULY 15.

TODAY thou shalt be with Me in Paradise.

MONDAY—JULY 16.

IF you've a heavy cross to bear you can try to get rid of it—and if you *do* get rid of it you'll never forgive yourself in all the years that follow. Or you can grow angry and bitter about it, and let the cross crush you.

Or you can carry it—just that, carry it bravely, without complaint, doing what has to be done, making the best of a bad job . . . and finding, to your astonishment, that somehow that cross becomes the glory of your life, and that—in fact—you are not carrying it at all, for God is bearing it for you.

TUESDAY—JULY 17.

AT all costs keep the love of at least a few folk.

Don't let trifles alienate you from husband or wife, son or daughter, the friend with whom you went to school. Keep such friendships in constant repair.

For the worst thing that can ever happen to us is that one day we may be alone—alone in the sense that nobody cares or wants to be bothered with us.

We live in a busy and a harassed world where most folk have so many worries of their own that unless they love us a lot they just haven't time to share our fears or even our joys.

It's so easy to be immersed in making money or carried away by some job or hobby, so easy to be touchy and thus to keep others at a distance . . . and then, when trouble comes, when illness or old age overtakes us, when bereavement robs us, to discover suddenly that we are nobody's concern.

So I repeat—At all costs keep the love of a few folk.

THE SUN IN TOWN

Oh what a difference when the sun comes out
And a rainbow in the fountain goes a winking round about.
The glossy pigeons cooing, fat and well-contented,
Inhabiting a happy world where time's not yet invented.

DAVID HOPE

GOLDEN MOMENTS

If Time would just stand still
For even a single day,
And all our perfect moments
Unchanged, unchanging stay!

But since we can't deny him,
  A memory we will light
To keep us faithful through the years
  To days of lost delight.

DAVID HOPE

THE LAST SHIFT

When I've worked my hindmost shift
And the hooters' voices lift,
Rousing folk from out their bed,
I'll be snug and warm instead.
Yet I know I'll lie and ponder
How they're getting on back yonder. . . . !

DAVID HOPE

THE FRIENDSHIP BOOK

> *I'M lucky being in hospital,*
> *Away from all the fuss.*
> *I take my ease in quietness . . .*
> *No need to catch a bus,*
> *Or rush to office, school or shop,*
> *Or wash the pots, or try*
> *To do ten thousand vexing things*
> *And breathless get—not I !*
> *I'm lucky resting here while you*
> *Have such a lot of jobs to do !*

THURSDAY—JULY 19.

HE was a kind of shaggy old lion limping across the floor in the common-room of a lodging-house.

I noticed him in particular because he was tall, though bent, and in spite of his age, long grey hair and the wildness in his eyes, there was a hint of splendour about him.

Somehow I was moved with compassion. I spoke to him and asked how he was. He looked at me suspiciously, turned his head, and refused to answer.

The chaplain told me the shabby giant had once had money and power, and that he had enjoyed the respect of many. One foolish move brought ruination, and thereafter a craving for drink had done the rest.

I confess that as I looked at that broken man, I was afraid . . . At this moment I have friends and a home, a job to do, the money I need, the respect of those about me. How careful I need be lest I, too, by a single folly ruin my own life and bring grief to others.

There, in that home of the homeless, I watched a fallen giant shuffling to his end ; and with all humility I said to myself: There, but for the grace of God, go I.

FRIDAY—JULY 20.

IT seems that a visitor to the town had decided to go to church, and had gone into a pew with a beautifully-upholstered cushion.

He had hardly been there two minutes when a couple came in and sat down in the same pew. They looked coldly at him, and then at each other. The man drew out a gold pencil and wrote something on a small slip of paper which he passed along to the visitor without so much as a word.

When the visitor unfolded it he read : " You are sitting in our seat." But he merely raised his eyebrows, wrote something beneath, and passed the slip of paper back, with a smile.

You can imagine the surprise when the paper was unfolded and the couple read his reply. The visitor had written : " And a jolly good seat it is, too !"

The best part of the story is that they just couldn't help smiling back after that.

SATURDAY—JULY 21.

I WISH I could take you to a small room in Wishart Memorial Church, Dundee.

In it a little group are gathered together. They are the kirk elders and the minister.

I'm told that every session meeting at Wishart Memorial begins with a short period of Bible study. The elders ask questions about any passage of the Bible they don't quite understand.

By these little discussions the elders are able to clear up points which the congregation bring to them, and they themselves get a fuller understanding.

I think everyone, at some time or other, has niggling doubts or difficulties about what they read in the Bible. This seems to me to be a fine way for those who guide our kirk to have these questions answered.

SUNDAY—JULY 22.

THOU shalt love thy neighbour as thyself.

MONDAY—JULY 23.

IN our youth we take the road with fair, untarnished dreams ; clean of heart and clean of hand, we make our splendid schemes.

Life sets hidden traps to snare the swift white feet of youth—many by-paths lead us from the narrow track of Truth.

Life goes on, temptations come, the road is rough and hard ; we struggle through the darkness, growing weary, worn and scarred. A moment comes when we must choose between the false and real—the way of self and safety or the way of the ideal.

Cling to this—no matter how the world may jibe and sneer ; lift your eyes to God's good skies, and keep the vision clear. Hold to something—something lovely, something pure and fine ; though the whole world fails you, keep your faith in things divine.

TUESDAY—JULY 24.

LAST year a friend was very upset by an unexpected bit of good fortune. I repeat the word *upset*.

She inherited two hundred pounds free of duty and it bothered her no end.

The bequest was from an old lady higher up the street, an old body to whom my friend had occasionally taken a wee gift, and with whom she had now and then had a chat. It seems that the lonely old soul had appreciated these little kindnesses far more than one might have thought . . . and when my friend came into that tidy legacy she kept saying, " Oh, I *wish* I'd done more for the old dear—I could have done it *so* easily !"

WEDNESDAY—JULY 25.

No use hoping for the moment
   When things are just so,
Sweet perfection never really
   Comes our way, you know.
You may dream romantic day-dreams,
   But life's common way
Has a snag or two to vex us . . .
   Seems it's made that way.
People who have mother-wit
Smile, and make the best of it.

THURSDAY—JULY 26.

I VISITED a factory employing hundreds of work-people—probably the jolliest crowd anywhere. Yet all of them were blind.

I marvelled at what I saw in this busy place.

I chatted with Margaret who was making brushes —and her clever fingers never once stopped work. I watched a man knocking nails into a piece of wood, a blind man who never hits his thumb.

There were men making brooms—applying boiling pitch with amazing skill. It seemed to me incredible that they could dip fibres into the bubbling pot without ever scalding their fingers. But they did.

Many of the employees I met sang or whistled while they worked, or cracked jokes ; and there was Willie, a craftsman in wood, who is a musician, and his friend, Alex., who plays at weddings and dances.

What's the point of all this? Not to enlist your sympathy for sightless men and women—maybe some of them get more out of life than we do.

The point is that if such folk can triumph over so great a handicap and keep on smiling, surely you and I ought to be able to put up with quite a lot of bother before we begin complaining.

FRIDAY—JULY 27.

WHAT is the lesson of childhood you have carried all through your life?

Mrs Elizabeth Forster will tell you that in her case it's the value of thrift and self-discipline.

Every Monday when she was a wee girl, Betty took a ha'penny to a friend who collected coppers for the penny bank.

After twelve exciting Mondays, lo and behold, she received a silver sixpence! It was a fortune beyond compare. Betty bought her mother three cups and saucers, and with the ha'penny left she started saving all over again.

Of course, that was nearly 50 years ago. Since then she has brought up four strapping sons and a daughter. She's never owed anybody a penny piece. And all along she has blessed the childhood thrill and lesson of thrift.

SATURDAY—JULY 28.

I WONDERED who on earth the Lady of the House was speaking to when I arrived home.

I opened the dining-room door and walked in.

There was her ladyship perched on the edge of the table—speaking to Coco, our neighbours' budgie! It seems the neighbours had gone on holiday and Coco was to stay with us till they come back.

We had him for only a few days—yet, incredibly, that tiny scrap of bright blue feathers stole our hearts.

From early morning, when the curtains were pulled back, till late at night, he chirped and swung and fluttered in his cage, telling us how glad he was to be alive and how nice it is to have someone to talk to.

What a godsend a budgie would be for some old folk who live alone . . . having him to come home to and discuss things with would be a tonic.

SUNDAY—JULY 29.

FORGIVE us our debts, as we also have forgiven our debtors.

MONDAY—JULY 30.

WHAT would *YOU* be prepared to do for your faith?

I know of a man who had a well-paid job in a coal mine. Because of the burning conviction of his creed he went to a lower-paid job so that he might be able to spread his faith among his fellow workers.

What is he—Protestant, Catholic, Methodist?

He is none of those. He is a Communist. But so deep are his beliefs that he is sacrificing his standard of living to further the cause he believes in.

Now I'm not suggesting we should all do as he did and throw up our jobs. But I am saying that his example presents a challenge no Christian can ignore.

TUESDAY—JULY 31.

SOME of you who own cars, and think nothing of a run may find it difficult to believe this :

I heard of an elderly body who was one of a party of pensioners which had a motor-coach tour among the bens and glens. She'd been the life of the party, but as the coach neared the city and the scene became familiar again she became very quiet.

And when she was out of the coach she turned impulsively to the driver, gave him a hug, and went away weeping. Somebody asked why. Her reply was " It's all been so wonderful !"

As I say, some of you may think all this nonsense . . . but folk who rarely or never " get away from it all " find exploring new scenes an almost over-whelmingly happy experience.

AUGUST

HOLIDAYS . . .jolly days,
    Nothing much to do ;
Laze about, in or out,
    As it pleases you.
Pray be kind, keep in mind
    Folk too weak for fun. . . .
Life is hard, drop a card,
    Share your bit of sun.

I SAT in the library and slowly turned the pages of a bulky book.

Each leaf was the size of a newspaper page and held the letters of St Paul. Yet I couldn't read one word !

Why? Because there was no writing as we know it. The pages were covered with rows and rows of tiny pimples no bigger than pin heads. There wasn't even a printed page number.

But what amazed me was how quickly my finger-tips discovered the different patterns made by the thousands of raised dots, and when I closed my eyes I sensed the message I knew was there.

You've guessed, of course. I was looking at part of the Bible in Braille—the key to the doors of blindness.

Louis Braille was a toddler of three when he blinded himself while playing in his father's saddler's shop near Paris. He was only 15 when he devised the ingenious system of dots that bears his name.

Today Braille is used all over the world and by 15,000 blind folk in Britain alone.

What a debt we owe to the man who not only triumphed over his own darkness, but has been such a blessing to others for over 100 years.

THE FRIENDSHIP BOOK

FRIDAY—AUGUST 3.

IT used to be called the poorshouse. . . .

There was no mistaking the high walls, the many windows and the little gate-house on the street. But, of course, I knew it wasn't the same place at all now.

Yet, as I walked into Orchard House Hospital, Stirling, I wondered what I would find. I never guessed it would be an angel.

For years Miss Wood's love and care were for babies. Now, as matron of Orchard House, her babies are the old, the worn out, the men and women with no place to go at journey's end.

I watched her chaff a crippled little man in a chair, and gently push back a lock of hair from his forehead. I knew then why it was he almost pined away when once he was moved to another home.

We spoke to old Will, whose brave old face is now but a shell, with one blind eye and one empty socket.

Yes, I do believe those who care for the old, as Miss Wood does, are the very salt of the earth.

SATURDAY—AUGUST 4.

YOUNG Ginger scrambled over the garden wall, pushed a scrap of paper in my hand and said, " Bet you can't solve this puzzle, Mr Gay."

Well, I've spent hours on the blessed thing—and it's got me beat. What do *you* make of it?

A man bought a bicycle for £30. Another two men wished to share the bicycle with him, so each paid £10. But the buyer, on paying cash, received a discount of £5. He gave each of the men £1 back, took £1 for himself and gave the other £2 to charity.

So now each man had paid £9 for the bicycle. Right? But if you add the three payments of £9, plus the £2 for charity, this comes to £29.

Puzzle is—where did the other £1 go?

IN THE PARK

A bench in the park,
A kindly bit sun.
Maybe the last
For summer's near done.

The papers are full
Of deeds that are dark,
But it's all far away
From my bench in the park.

DAVID HOPE

THE HILLMAN'S WISH

Oh, to walk the hills once more
  By little paths I know,
To climb where hawk and eagle soar
  And clouds go wheeling slow !
To smell bog myrtle's healing balm
  And in the rushing wind find calm.

DAVID HOPE

SUNDAY—AUGUST 5.

HE that receiveth a prophet in the name of a prophet shall receive a prophet's reward ; and he that receiveth a righteous man in the name of a righteous man shall receive a righteous man's reward. And whosoever shall give to drink unto one of these little ones a cup of cold water only, in the name of a disciple, verily I say unto you, he shall in no wise lose his reward.

MONDAY—AUGUST 6.

THE Lady of the House thinks it's the best holiday idea she's ever heard of !

You'll understand why when I tell you about Craigengower, the Women's Home Mission holiday house at Tighnabruaich, a stone's throw from the waters of the Kyles of Bute.

But it's not just special because of its beautiful setting. It's such a blessing to womenfolk, too.

For instance, it's a place tired mothers can go for a whole week's rest, away from family worries and the thousand and one little things they must remember to do every day in the year.

It's a place for old bodies, who perhaps have lived in a single room all their days and have never known surroundings other than dusty city streets.

The splendid thing is that everything is taken care of for the visitors to Craigengower.

The women are looked after like queens by their kirk sisters and deaconesses, and all the cooking, cleaning, scrubbing and dusting is done by volunteers.

No wonder the Lady of the House is taken with the idea. She insists I also say that when the time comes for the women to go home again, they may find they're appreciated that little bit more by their husbands and families !

TUESDAY—AUGUST 7.

ONCE upon a time there was an old Scotswoman who would rather have died than miss a kirk service on the Sabbath.

Which was why she battled so magnificently against the wind one very stormy morning. The wind was in her face all the time, but she kept on till she arrived, late and puffed, but triumphant.

She couldn't help thinking about the return journey, so the minute she had breath to spare, she prayed that the wind wouldn't change.

But the wind did change—all the way home it was dead against her !

It's an old story, with a chuckle in it. And there's something more.

In these days no end of folk don't believe in prayer. I do. But so often God would be unkind if He answered our prayers in the way we want them answered.

What you and I need to do is to pray for strength to endure, humility to follow God's guidance, courage to dare, patience to wait . . and to such as ask for spiritual blessings, God answers in ways far more miraculous than many people believe to be possible.

WEDNESDAY—AUGUST 8.

IN this old world, so mad and bad,
There's much we must deplore—
No end of fears and griefs and pains,
And follies by the score.
But saints and angels walk our streets,
And kindly folk we meet ;
There are unnumbered lovely things,
And deeds both brave and sweet.
Let this be all our daily quest :
To find (and talk about) the best !

THURSDAY—AUGUST 9.

HAVE you heard about the American tourist who was " doing " Scotland last summer, and came —guide book in hand—to Dunkeld, where he rushed around in next to no time, but felt he really must pause a moment on the bridge.

One of Dunkeld's oldest inhabitants happened to be there, smoking his pipe, looking at the water flowing by, and thinking about nothing.

" Say," purred the rich American, " this is a swell town, eh?"

The Scotsman nodded.

" Any really big guys born here?"

" No," was the quick reply. " Only children."

FRIDAY—AUGUST 10.

I WAS in London a few hours last week—only a few hours. About noon, on a gloriously sunny day, I found myself within ten minutes' walk of St Paul's. As I turned a corner I spotted a very dark-skinned road-sweeper—black woolly hair, chocolate-brown skin, teeth shining like pearls. He was pushing a barrow. His eyes were turned upwards—he had simply no regard for the traffic roaring by.

As I passed I heard him singing: " Hi, hi! I'm happy as the sky!"

" Haven't you any troubles?" I inquired.

He beamed. " Me plenny trouble, mistah," said he. " No see ma wife and little ones this long time. But the sun's shining, Mistah . . . why worry?"

Then off he went, trundling his barrow, and still singing, " Hi, hi! I'm happy as the sky!"

I thought at first what a simpleton he was ; but long before I reached St Paul's I was wondering if, after all, I were the simpleton, he the wise man making the best of whatever good he found.

SATURDAY—AUGUST 11.

HAVE you ever heard the story of Albert and Franz Durer?

They were brothers who lived in Germany and, although they were very poor, they both wanted to be artists.

So the younger one, Albert, said to Franz—" I've an idea—I'll work as a labourer and pay for your training. Then when you're finished you can do the same for me "

" Fine," said Franz. " But we'll do it my way. You go and study first and I'll work." For he knew his brother's talents were far greater than his own.

So it was. For years Albert studied under the finest masters of his day, while Franz toiled to pay the cost.

At last Albert returned and joyously greeted his brother. " Now you'll be able to go, Franz," he cried.

But silently Franz held up his hands. Alas, they were no longer the hands of an artist, but the hands of a workman . . . so gnarled with years of labour that they weren't even able to hold a pencil.

Albert stared at them wordlessly and put his arm round his brother's shoulders. With tears in his eyes he said, " Franz, I can repay you in only one way— I shall draw a picture that will speak to men's hearts —a picture of these hands of sacrifice and love."

Today, 400 years later, the picture of the praying hands is, of course, known the world over—immortalised in a brother's tribute.

SUNDAY—AUGUST 12.

ASK, and it shall be given you ; seek, and ye shall find ; knock, and it shall be opened unto you : For every one that asketh receiveth ; and he that seeketh findeth ; and to him that knocketh it shall be opened.

MONDAY—AUGUST 13.

I WAS amused the other day when a friend showed me a really wonderful collection of coloured snaps of Rotterdam. She and her husband had been staying a few days with some Dutch friends who live five or six miles out of the city, and every day the two of them had invaded Rotterdam with a camera.

I say I was amused—not at the pictures, but at the remark the lady made. " They've come out well, haven't they?" she asked. Before I could agree she went on, " And; you know, the funny thing is this. We sent a copy of each of the best snaps to our Dutch friends—and the other morning we had a letter from them saying they'd had no idea Rotterdam was such a colourful and interesting place, and all of them were going to have a fresh look at it!"

As I have confessed, that amused me . . . and it made me think too. How many things well worth seeing am I missing each day just because I am so familiar with them?

TUESDAY—AUGUST 14.

I ASKED a number of people if they could say what Amen means, and almost all told me it was a kind of full-stop. One young scholar assured me it was an old Hebrew word meaning " It is finished." " That's why it's tacked on at the end of some of our hymns," he added.

But he misses the point. Amen means " So be it. Verily, it is so !" Sometimes it indicates our consent or agreement.

A week ago I found myself singing in church :

Take my life, and let it be
Consecrated, Lord, to Thee. . . .

And when we sang the Amen, I wondered at my own courage. Did I really dare to say, " So be it "?

WEDNESDAY—AUGUST 15.

IT'S little things—a lone thrush sings,
 A pleasant tea for two,
A story told, a hand to hold,
 A child who worships you.
A memory dear of yesteryear,
 A gossip in the street.
A bit of fun, sight of the sun,
 A rest for tired feet. . . .
It's little things like these each day
 Which cheer the pilgrim on his way.

THURSDAY—AUGUST 16.

NOW why did the Lady of the House choose a window table in the restaurant?

There's only one answer : *To see the view.* She could sit by the upstairs window and admire the flowers in the window-box and look out across the busy street to the colourful gardens.

Two minutes later she was joined by a couple of elderly dears, one wearing very thick spectacles, the other blind.

They talked to each other like budgerigars on a branch—the almost blind lady ordering for the completely blind one. The Lady of the House lent a hand, and all three had a heart to heart chat.

Between the second and third courses the lady with the spectacles peered out of the window and did her best to describe to the blind woman what there was to see. She herself mistook trees for houses, however !

They were a gay and gallant pair, these two elderly sisters . . . and they taught the Lady of the House something : That every day she ought to thank God for eyes to see the beauty and the colour and wonder of this world. Supposing *she'd* gone to lunch . . . and couldn't see beyond the window !

FRIDAY—AUGUST 17.

A UNIVERSITY professor said: "In spite of all they tried to teach me at school and at the university, it was an old shepherd who gave me one of the best pieces of advice I've ever had.

"He said that in the daytime we should read the forgettable and at night the unforgettable."

I am not sure I understood this immediately, but as the professor went on talking I began to see how profound this really is—Read something of what is current to keep abreast with today's events and thought, but read also the timeless books which buttress the mind against hasty conclusions and enrich the spirit with immovable truth.

In life there's room for the ridiculous—but there ought to be room also for the sublime.

SATURDAY—AUGUST 18.

WE were a very small company following the hearse along the path in the churchyard, and a friend and I found ourselves in step at the end of the little procession. We said nothing at first. Then my friend glanced at me. "It'll be a new experience for Jim—being at the front for once," said he in low tones, nodding towards the coffin. "He always put himself last, you know."

It was then I allowed myself to smile.

Yet how true it was. For all his long life that was the chief characteristic of the man who is mourned by all who knew him.

Always he put others first—his parents, his wife, his children, friends and neighbours. He might have won fame and made money if only he had paid less attention to other people's feelings and looked after his own interests. He might have done more and gone farther. But he could never have been happier.

SUNDAY—AUGUST 19.

NOT every one that saith unto Me, Lord, Lord, shall enter into the kingdom of heaven , but he that doeth the will of My Father which is in heaven.

MONDAY—AUGUST 20.

COULD any father have done more?

Just after the war the Rev Andrew Burnett became the father of a baby girl. She was the apple of his eye.

Only one thing marred his happiness. His health was failing, and he feared he might pass on before his little girl grew up. So he decided, if that ever happened, he would leave behind something by which she might feel his guiding presence in her life.

What could he leave that would help his little girl most in later years? He decided to write a book.

Of course, it was to be no ordinary book. It would be the story of his life—his ambitions and ideals, his faith and philosophy. So, while she played happily at his feet in his study, Mr Burnett sat and wrote out the book of his life—from his childhood to his work in the ministry, his marriage, and his crowning joy, the birth of his baby girl.

He told her, too, of his hopes and prayers for her, and of this last bequest he made to her.

But even before he could finish his work he died suddenly, leaving his little daughter with only the book to remember him by.

Over the years since then she has read and re-read her father's story, and each time she learns something more about him, and of the secret of living.

Today, as a girl in her teens, she still has the book. She tries to live by it and still finds wonderful inspiration in it, for it contains all the riches of experience of a father she was too young to know.

TUESDAY—AUGUST 21.

HE began doing one thing—and ended by doing the opposite.

A pretty tough guy born in Indiana in 1827, he had a share of fighting in the Mexican War and in the American Civil War Though he became a major-general, he had a flair for politics and travel—but he was happiest when writing books.

He began writing a book after talking with a friend. " Who can believe in all the nonsense they teach in churches?" he demanded.

" Nobody," his friend agreed, adding, " You ought to write a book to prove that no such man as Jesus Christ ever lived. It would make you famous."

So the tough guy sat down and wrote the first four chapters of a book to prove that Christianity is a myth   and while he wrote his wife was praying that her husband would see the light of truth.

Late one night her husband opened the door and said, " Christ did live—and Christ does live!"

Then he rewrote the first four chapters, and went on to finish the book, " Ben-Hur."

Strange that Lew Wallace should scorn Christ, and that in trying to prove that the Saviour was a myth he succeeded in enthroning Him not only in his own heart but in the hearts of others!

WEDNESDAY—AUGUST 22.

MR MEANT-TO has a comrade,
 And his name is Didn't-Do.
Have you ever chanced to meet them?
 Have they ever called on you?
These two fellows live together
 In the house of Never-Seen ,
And I'm told that it is haunted
 By the ghost of Might-Have-Been.

THURSDAY—AUGUST 23.

A STERN, grey-bearded man sat in the study of a chill, rambling manse in Islington.

His hands strayed idly over the keys of the piano.

Outside the wind howled and rattled the windows. The gas light flickered with each gust.

But the man in the minister's collar at the piano didn't seem to notice. His thoughts were back in his native Aberdeenshire, to the rolling hills he'd played among as a lad.

As he sat he hummed under his breath. And the tune he hummed that night has gone gloriously round the world.

" Immortal, invisible, God only wise,
  In light inaccessible hid from our eyes.   ."

Little did the Rev. Walter Chalmers Smith guess as he wrote those words nearly a hundred years ago that his hymn would become dear to us all.

FRIDAY—AUGUST 24.

THIS little story is about Miss Margaret, who has a little flat all her own—rather cheaper than you might expect because it is near some smoky chimneys and you have to dust the sideboard twice a day at least.

For years that has been Miss Margaret's one complaint—twice a day she has had to dust her sideboard. The dust and smoke, carried by the wind, get into her small room, and she's for ever dusting.

Then she was taken ill. They rushed her to hospital, operated, and kept her in the ward week after week.

And there was only one thing Miss Margaret wanted . to get back to her flat *and do the dusting!* Over and over she told the Lady of the House : " Oh, if only I was back and could dust my sideboard twice a day. . . I'd be perfectly happy ! I would really ! I'm just longing to dust my sideboard !"

SATURDAY—AUGUST 25.

WHEN asked by a disciple for a rule of life, Confucius replied, " Do not unto others what you would not they should do unto you."

SUNDAY—AUGUST 26.

THE Lord is my shepherd ; I shall not want. He maketh me to lie down in green pastures : He leadeth me beside the still waters. He restoreth my soul : He guideth me in the paths of righteousness for His name's sake.

MONDAY—AUGUST 27.

THE Whitmore family saw it when they were on holiday in the Highlands . . . a sight you would be lucky to see once in a lifetime.

As they drove towards the Commando memorial at Spean Bridge they drew up to pay homage, and they were impressed, as everyone is, by the three silent soldiers gazing over the distant moors as if they could see something that no mortal eyes can see.

Then, before the Whitmores' very eyes, a brilliant rainbow began to form. Faintly at first, yet growing brighter every second, it stretched from the valley beneath, above the heads of the three soldiers, until it dipped down again, curving away into the glen.

The onlookers held their breath in wonder. The rugged statues seemed to be right in the centre of a halo from heaven.

Just as gradually as it appeared, the rainbow began to fade—until it had vanished, leaving the Whitmores wondering if it had all been a dream.

I am sure they will agree with me that in moments like these, the hand of the Creator seems to pass over us like a benediction.

TUESDAY—AUGUST 28.

THE pretty little nurse assured the Lady of the House she'd *love* to come and have tea with us one afternoon—but it wasn't easy to arrange a convenient time. She was on night duty.

When she did come she was altogether charming. We were both sorry when she had to " run along."

I ran her back to the nurses' hostel, and she gave me a fascinating smile as she waved " Good-bye." And all the way home I was thinking about our little nurse . . . diminutive and delicate (or so it seemed), but used to hard work, accepting heavy responsibility as a matter of course, doing her duty conscientiously —and often going the second mile.

Odd to think that when I went to bed that night our teenager nurse was on duty all through the small hours, seeing to things, lending a hand, doing her stuff . . . and doing it all efficiently and beautifully.

I write about this because it's so easy to live year after year and never once think about what goes on at night while we are snug abed . . . nurses and doctors, policemen, sailors, post office workers. Such a lot of folk at work while you and I rest.

Nice to say " Thank you " to them, isn't it?

WEDNESDAY—AUGUST 29.

FEELING life has hit you hard,
Knocked you flat as flat?
Gone your hopes of love and joy—
Finished with all that?
You're not beaten yet, not you,
Not a little bit !
Scorn whatever ill is yours—
You can deal with it !
Patience, courage, plod and grin. . . .
Keep on fighting till you win.

THURSDAY—AUGUST 30.

HAVE you ever stopped to think that you can't see the wonders of the heavens at night when there are lamps on every side and shop windows ablaze?

You see the stars best on a dark, clear, moonless night . . . when you're far from any buildings.

The idea also occurs to me that when all goes well, when we are enjoying good health and everybody can afford plenty of pleasures, it's difficult to see God— the brightness all around hides Him because we have, it would seem, so little need of Him.

But when the lights go out, and when you and I are walking alone in the blackness of our sorrow or distress or fear . . . how wonderfully bright and near God can seem then, how glad and thankful we are to be assured that if we put ourselves in His hands He will guide us all the way !

FRIDAY—AUGUST 31.

CALLING Mrs Helen Sheldon's dad !

If anybody deserves a cheer—it's you !

How do I know? It's simple—I had a letter from your daughter Helen in Brisbane, Australia, asking me to say how much you mean to all your family.

Although you were badly wounded in the First War, Dad, and were left paralysed down one side, you kept on working as a glazier until you retired after 53 years' service. During that time you've stood out in all weathers, on frosty rooftops and snow-filled parks and streets, fixing broken panes of glass.

Often you found it hard to manage the glass on your " one good side," as you call it. Yet, like the good soldier you are, you never even thought of giving in.

Francis Gay dips his flag to you, sir—and to all the other dads like you who give so willingly, yet ask so little in return.

SEPTEMBER

WHEN Dr Hugh Douglas was on a motoring holiday in the Highlands, he was struck by the fact that on every dangerous bend and at the bottom of steep hills was a pile of coarse sand. Beside it was a notice which said, " Grit—for roads."

That phrase remained in Dr Douglas's mind. So much so that when he came to give a broadcast sermon, he took it as his theme. . . . When you hit a bad patch, when you can't seem to get going or when you begin to slide—draw on the hidden reserve of strength labelled " Grit for roads."

It so happened that listening to his broadcast that day was a man who had just been told he had six months to live. Everything had seemed so rosy and now his whole world was shattered.

But as he listened to the minister's words, he determined he would spend the last six months of his life as happily as he had spent his earlier years . . . and he did.

A year later, Dr Douglas by chance met the man's wife. She told the minister that her husband had remembered his words to the day he died.

But what I think was even more remarkable was that when her husband passed on she received many letters of sympathy and the one which did most to strengthen and comfort her was a short message from a close friend, which said simply—" Remember, grit for roads."

BLESSED is the man that walketh not in the counsel of the wicked, nor standeth in the way of sinners, nor sitteth in the seat of the scornful.

MONDAY—SEPTEMBER 3.

THE McBay family were on their way home from a holiday in Wales. It was raining heavily, and they couldn't find anywhere to stay the night.

At length they reached Airdrie and stopped at a house with a "Bed and Breakfast" sign. But the landlady could take only two of the family, so Mrs McBay and her daughter stayed there, while Mr McBay and his son tried to find other accommodation.

But it was no use. They would need to sleep in the car. There wasn't a bed in all Airdrie, or so it seemed.

That's when Tom Morris appeared out of the blue. The McBays were total strangers to him, yet he offered them the use of his mother's house, as she was away on holiday. He directed the men to the house, gave them the choice of two beds, and said that before they left just to pop the keys in his letter-box across the road. And he wouldn't dream of taking a penny

Three cheers for Tom Morris.

TUESDAY—SEPTEMBER 4.

I PICK out the following as the most significant letter I have received for a long, long time :—

" Last week, with my sister-in-law, I went for a week's holiday. We shared a room, which had two single beds in it.

" Before retiring to bed every night my sister-in-law knelt down to say her prayers.

" You see, although I am a Methodist and a Christian by profession, my prayers are sadly lacking, while my sister-in-law, who does not profess anything regarding church-going, did this. . .

" Often I had wondered why everybody loved her and why she had such a kind, courageous, yet courteous disposition. Now I know where her source of strength and kindness comes from."

WEDNESDAY—SEPTEMBER 5.

I'VE chores to do, the same as you
(And bother the chores, I say).
But wet or dry, the bairns and I
Have a bright spot every day :
The table's laid ; the toast is made—
You've guessed what the thrill must be?
Life's rich again the moment when
Daddy comes home to tea !

THURSDAY—SEPTEMBER 6.

IMAGINE a big housing estate, only half completed. The ground is churned into a mire of mud and the few roads there are peter out into a rough track.

It was to such a place that the Rev. John Stewart and his wife went.

There was no kirk, no manse, not even a congregation. Indeed, there were only two names on the roll— his wife's and his own. But, undaunted, Mr Stewart buckled to.

He found a cottage and turned it into a manse. As there wasn't a church he emptied the furniture out of his front room and put in 40 chairs and a piano. And as there was no congregation he simply went out and knocked on every door he came to !

Soon his room was full to overflowing. So what do you think? He got the use of other front rooms in the homes of his new members until he was taking as many as nine services on a Sunday.

Now Mr Stewart has a fine hall-church, and there's a whisper he might be getting a bigger kirk for his parish soon. He has a membership of over a thousand, a thriving Sunday School and Bible class, and as fine a group of elders as you could meet.

Yet it all began with two people, a little cottage— and a great faith.

SERVICE

Beyond the glitter and the crown
The splendour we observe,
From generations handed down
Shines forth the will to serve.

DAVID HOPE

A NICE CUP OF TEA

I like it at my breaktime,
By the fireside at night,
In fact there's no occasion
When a "cuppa" isn't right!

DAVID HOPE

FRIDAY—SEPTEMBER 7.

WHEN May was in love with Arthur—oh, my goodness, what a paragon he was. Arthur was perfection personified. Arthur was the faultless knight, the mirror of chivalry. . . .

But when a new young man came into May's ken, Arthur was instantly out of favour—and what a host of weaknesses May saw in him . . . so ill-dressed, so thoughtless, so boorish, so selfish, so opinionated. Indeed, Arthur deserved nothing less than hanging.

What a silly thing May must be.

It's a good thing you and I are not like May, isn't it?

SATURDAY—SEPTEMBER 8.

IF you happened to peep over the shoulder of the Rev. T. W. Jarvie, you might have noticed he was writing out questions on little slips of paper.

They were questions like these—" Is God alive?" . . . " Is there a hell?" . . . " Is it really essential to be ' converted ' before you can be a Christian?" . . . " Is the Church out of date?"

Difficult questions to answer, you might observe, and I would agree with you. Yet Mr Jarvie wasn't noting them down for his sermon. You see, recently he conducted a seaside mission at Prestwick, and with him were young folk from all over Scotland who gave up their holidays to help.

Each of them was handed a slip and asked to think about the question on it. Then one after another, they stood up on a box on the crowded beach, and in their own way answered the question.

Earnestness shone in their faces, and their words were strengthened by the conviction of their own faith.

I know that more than a few holidaymakers at Prestwick had their faith refreshed by the young folk who had the courage to stand up and speak.

SUNDAY—SEPTEMBER 9.

BUT Thou, O Lord, art a shield about me.

MONDAY—SEPTEMBER 10.

WHAT'S the greatest weakness any one can have. An odd—perhaps rather a disturbing—question, isn't it? How would *you* answer it? Would you say lying or being boastful? Would you say heavy drinking or bad living or interfering in other people's business or being lazy?

Thomas Carlyle had his views on the matter. He declared : " The greatest of faults, I should say, is to be conscious of none."

TUESDAY—SEPTEMBER 11.

MORNING after morning an old lady looks for the postman, hoping. Morning after morning the postman goes by, or, if he calls, he fails to bring the one letter which would set this gallant lady's heart ablaze.

There's the simplest story behind this tragedy— father and son didn't get on. Maybe the father was much too domineering. Maybe the son was self-opinionated. Who can tell the rights and wrongs? The upshot was the son packed his things and walked out of the house in a temper.

That was eight years ago . . . and he has never been heard of since. Meanwhile, his father has died.

You see, of course, what has happened? A mother, innocent as the day, is the one who suffers. But now she is bereft of husband and son . . . and how she *longs* to see her boy again, to hear his voice, to know if all is well, to share in his successes or sorrows. . . .

Sad it is to suffer when you have done wrong. How much sadder to suffer when all you have done is to keep on loving year after year . . .

WEDNESDAY—SEPTEMBER 12.

FROM the fields and gardens now
Richness comes, we know not how.
Fruits and grain once more appear,
Crowning all the varied year.
Toil and patience—but for these
Who'd be reaping, if you please?
You and I, as well we know,
Harvest only what we sow.

THURSDAY—SEPTEMBER 13.

COME back with me a moment to the turn of the century . . . a laddie is running home from school. As he passes a shop, he pauses, looks in the window, and goes inside to spend his Saturday ha'penny.

Perhaps it was the first time young Albert Orsborn had met Mother Shepherd, the good soul who had the shop. But it certainly wasn't the last.

When you went into Mother Shepherd's, you got so much more than just the liquorice strips or sugar mice that filled the bottles on her shelves. She had a wonderful way of putting high things into lowly language, so that children always understood her.

So, often, after school came out, she sat behind her counter and talked to Albert . . . about the Bible . . . about what he'd learned at Sunday school . . . about the fish he'd caught . . . about all manner of things. It was almost as if she knew he was destined for great things.

Albert never forgot Mother Shepherd. Indeed, her influence led him into the Salvation Army, where he rose to become its General.

The General has been retired for several years now— but he still remembers Mother Shepherd in her wee shop; the old body who, in a a way, marched steadfastly beside him through a lifetime's crusading.

FRIDAY—SEPTEMBER 14.

HUNDREDS of years ago, a young lad and his old grandfather sat by a burn high in the hills of the north. The old man was teaching the boy to play the bagpipes, and as they sat a great stag broke from a nearby thicket, and stood still as a statue.

The sun shone on its russet coat, and its curved, branching antlers were held high and steady. Suddenly the stag went off like the wind, leaping from boulder to boulder with unbelievable grace until it disappeared.

" Ay, laddie," said the old man, " ye canna leap like that !"

The boy didn't reply. Instead, he rose to his feet and began to dance. His arms were stretched above his head, his fingers pointing like the antlers of the red deer. When his toes touched the heather, they were light as thistledown. The old man was so excited he reached for his pipes, and soon the Highland Fling skirled over the hills for the first time.

As the years passed, the boy grew into manhood. Wherever he went, he was asked to dance the Dance of the Stag, and, as others learned it, it became known far and wide, until at length it formed part of the heritage of Scotland.

SATURDAY—SEPTEMBER 15.

YOU cannot think straight when you are upset, worried and anxious. At such times try, if possible, to keep this truth at the back of your mind.

Things have gone wrong, you have had a shock, your mind is in a whirl. . . depend on it, you have a one-sided view of the matter ; you are approaching it from the wrong angle ; you've an exaggerated notion of it. It's so easy to do or say the wrong thing, and regret it later ; so easy to think there's no way out.

If, therefore, you've a problem : *sleep on it !*

SUNDAY—SEPTEMBER 16.

HEARKEN unto the voice of my cry, my King, and my God : for unto Thee do I pray.

MONDAY—SEPTEMBER 17.

SINCE Janet was a young girl she has been compelled to live in her wheelchair, for she cannot walk a step. Yet, long ago, she made up her mind there was only one thing to do—make the best of it.

Janet looks after her mother, who's well over 80 now. She dusts the house and even polishes the floors. She cooks all the meals for herself and her mother, and her sister and her two girls who live there, too, On top of that there's mending, washing, scrubbing —all done from the wheelchair.

On a Friday night she's wheeled to the handicapped folks' club and there she spends the only few hours off that she allows herself.

What's her secret? It's simple. " You can't live on sympathy," she says. She always takes life as she finds it, and in doing so she has become one of the most contented women I know.

TUESDAY—SEPTEMBER 18.

EDWARD DYER, a poet, passed on nearly 360 years ago. What in the world could he say in that far-off time to be of interest to us in this day and generation? Here's what he said—as true now as in his day :—

Some have too much, yet still do crave.
I little have, and seek no more.
They are but poor though much they have,
And I am rich with little store.
They poor, I rich ; they beg, I give.
They lack, I have ; they pine, I live.

WEDNESDAY—SEPTEMBER 19.

IF you can say a friendly word,
  Or give a bit of cheer,
Or help somebody in their need,
  Or wipe away a tear . . .
Today's the day to get it done—
  Don't let your good deed wait;
Now is your chance. What if you find
  Tomorrow is too late ?

THURSDAY—SEPTEMBER 20.

YEARS ago Mrs Holliday had an invalid husband to nurse, seven children of their own to bring up, and two orphans she had taken in. Yet, all she had in the house was a bag of lentils and a threepenny bit.

Goodness knows, she had had her troubles before, but there was no blacker day than that.

With her threepence in her purse she went to the butcher for a bone, and he, good man, gave her not just one bone but a whole big bowlful.

If ever better days began in a stranger way, I've yet to hear of them. . . .

Back home, Mrs Holliday put the bones in her big copper boiler, emptied in all the lentils, and made the biggest pot of soup she'd ever laid eyes on. Enough to feed a regiment, you'd say.

And that's just about what Mrs Holliday did, for after feeding her family she sold the rest of the soup round the miners' homes. With the money she bought meat and flour and made pies . . . then potted meat, then bread, and—hey, presto !—soon she had her own shop and could earn enough to bring up her big family and care for her husband.

Mrs Holliday is retired now, plump and motherly, and you would never guess she had the grit of half a dozen women. " I had God's help," is what she'll say.

AT this season of the year, when so many people are
on the move, travelling near and far, adventur-
ing at home or under foreign skies, let us remember
that old, old Scottish tale of the wee laddie who lived
in a very small house in a sheltered valley miles from
anywhere. "Oh," exclaimed the boy every day of
his life, "if only I could travel and see the world!
If only I could see the world!"

So he sighed. Thus he spoke.

And the years went by and he grew to be a man and
became representative for a big firm of wholesalers
. . . spending the greater part of every year travelling
in Europe and America, and sometimes in India and
China and Northern Africa . . . thousands upon
thousands of miles, meeting hundreds of people, seeing all the great and wonderful sights of more than
half the cities of the world. . . .

And always in his heart, deep in his heart, was a
longing, an urgent, insistent longing to live in a small
house in a lonely valley, and there to smoke a pipe of
peace.

SATURDAY—SEPTEMBER 22.

WAS I hungry? The time was after six-thirty when
I reached home, and I had missed lunch because
of this and that. Indoors I went, calling out, "Hello?
I'm famished!"

"Ah," murmured the Lady of the House, address-
ing one of her old dears, "here's Francis. He'll run
you home . . . the long way round!"

I obeyed orders, took Miss Roberts a run in the
evening sunshine, and didn't get back till ten to
eight . . . but what a tea was waiting me—and such a
warm little hug!

Nice (if naughty) to feel saintly, isn't it?

SUNDAY—SEPTEMBER 23.

I WILL give thanks unto the Lord according to His righteousness : and will sing praise to the name of the Lord Most High.

MONDAY—SEPTEMBER 24.

I WAS in church for the morning service. The Rev. Scott Hutchison was the preacher.

He came into the church from the vestry on crutches. When he reached the pulpit steps he put the crutches down, turned his body right round and levered himself backwards, step by step, up into the pulpit.

Mr Hutchison was serving in the army in India after the war when polio struck him down. One moment he played rugby and tennis, and was at the peak of fitness. Six hours later, with no more warning than a twinge like lumbago, his legs were paralysed. They still are.

How does a man, not yet thirty, with the best of life ahead, stand up to such a blow? Mr Hutchison, undaunted, answered the question by studying for the ministry. Nothing would stop him then—and nothing has stopped him since.

For six years now he has been a minister in the fullest sense of the word. Callers at the manse are received by a beaming, sturdy figure in a wheelchair. A hand-controlled car takes him round his parish. And as the Kirk's chaplain to overseas students, he has even made a visit to Ghana !

I ask you, could any man do more in overcoming such a crippling disability?

It was a splendid sermon Mr Hutchison gave us. But even more, I will remember the man who walked into the pulpit backwards—the man who built a full life of service when it seemed his whole world had collapsed about him.

TUESDAY—SEPTEMBER 25.

RECENTLY a handful of teachers in a Sunday school visited hundreds of houses, having a friendly chat with no end of people.

Their job was to invite parents to send their children to Sunday school.

What was the result of this campaign?

Not one name was added to the list. Those teachers had knocked at doors, said their pieces, handed in their leaflets, all to no purpose.

What interests me so much is not that the campaign was a failure, *but that those Sunday school teachers are shortly to knock at the same doors again !*

They're not intimidated by failure. They haven't lost hope. Any day now they'll be going the rounds once more.

That, of course, is what the Church has been doing for nearly 2000 years. People make fun of it. They ignore it. They try to destroy it. No matter, the few who believe keep on keeping on, worshipping, praying, singing, hoping . . . and always trying to win the hearts and loyalties of men and women.

For this remains true—with all its faults, the Church is the truest revelation of God's will and purpose . . . and its faithful lovers never tire of trying to draw others into its fellowship.

WEDNESDAY—SEPTEMBER 26.

GONE are the long, bright summer days ;
Now autumn fires glow.
Soon, soon the trees will shed their leaves
And colder winds will blow.
But what care I what ills and chills
The coming days may bring?
There never was a winter yet
Which did not turn to spring.

THURSDAY—SEPTEMBER 27.

WE were all talking at once as we went into the farmhouse kitchen, but as we sat down to tea silence fell upon us, and in that silence our host said grace.

Afterwards I remarked that not many folk in these days say grace.

" No—and more's the pity," replied the old farmer. " Mebbe, if after they'd ploughed and sown and harrowed and waited for corn to spring up and reach maturity they would stop to think how little man does to produce it, and what a big hand in harvest God has. They'd realise that bread's a miracle. Mebbe then they'd give thanks before daring to eat it."

FRIDAY—SEPTEMBER 28.

MR JAMES FREW has passed to his rest. Many lovely flowers were sent in tribute, but I think the most beautiful was a simple spray inscribed, " From the flowers in your garden."

The flowers came from the local children. They had given their pocket money for a loving farewell to the man who was " Grandpa " to them all.

Jim was truly one of God's messengers, for he had the gift of friendship to a wonderful degree, and his greatest love of all was for children.

Not long ago he was walking up the street with some friends when one of them drew his attention to a crowd of children in his garden. " They'll ruin all your flowers, Jim," remarked the friend.

Jim's reply was typical—" Don't worry about that. The children are the real flowers in my garden."

Many a man far greater in the world's esteem would, I am sure, be proud if, at the end of life's journey, he could say he had won the hearts of children as Jim Frew had done.

SATURDAY—SEPTEMBER 29.

WHEN we do a kindness, little do we think how long it will be remembered by others.

For example, Mr Thomas tells me of an experience during the war, when he was serving in a flying-boat escorting convoys across the Atlantic. On their way back from one trip, their plane was forced down at Benbecula.

Now the men had been flying for over 20 hours non-stop. And, after an emergency meal, Mr Thomas and his ten comrades longed more than anything for a cigarette. But to their dismay, they hadn't one between them, and after trying almost every shop in the place they were still out of luck.

Then Mr Thomas spotted a wee shop in the square. It sold mostly ironmongery, but as a last resort he went in.

With a quiet nod, the old shopkeeper went into the back shop and came back with a shoe box. " How many cigarettes would you be wanting?" he asked.

Mr Thomas said, hopefully, they would be thankful for even 20 to share amongst them. Whereupon the old man pushed the shoe-box over and said simply, " You take the box. It's a Christmas present."

Mr Thomas looked down at the box . . . It was crammed with over 500 loose cigarettes ! And it was only when he was outside he realised Christmas was still four months away !

Only some cigarettes, but 11 men will never forget the old Islander who gave them so willingly when they were needed most.

SUNDAY—SEPTEMBER 30.

JESUS said unto him, No man, having put his hand to the plough, and looking back, is fit for the kingdom of God.

OCTOBER

ONE day a big ocean liner was being launched. A famous lady smashed the bottle of champagne against the bows, and everyone waited for the vessel to slide smoothly down into the water.

But it refused to budge! In the hubbub that followed, someone jokingly cried—" Give it a shove, somebody!"—and a boy ran forward and put his shoulder against the great liner's bows!

Of course, there was a great shout of laughter—but it soon changed to applause. For slowly the ship began to slip away, until it took the water. It seems the balance of the ship had been so delicate, it took only the gentle push of a boy's shoulder to start it off.

I don't know where this happened, or even if it happened. But I do know that when we're tempted to say, " But what can *I* do on my own?" we should remember the story of the boy and the liner.

TUESDAY—OCTOBER 2.

I LIKE the old story of a Scotsman who had the misfortune to lose his sight and both legs in a colliery accident.

He had been a very active man, and folk thought he would pine away. But he kept on being as cheery as ever—and people said it was a delight to hear his hearty laughter.

Some years later a minister called to see the blind cripple. " You've suffered terribly," he murmured.

" Yes," agreed the miner, " it was a bad do while it lasted—but there are compensations, you know. One is I never suffer from cold feet nowadays ; and another is that I can read my Braille books in the dark. *I've a mighty lot to be thankful for.*"

WEDNESDAY—OCTOBER 3.

NOW woods are silent—one by one
The brown leaves fall till all are gone ;
The garden glory fades, and chill
Blows autumn's breath across the hill.
Yet in the sunset glow, I hear
The sweet, brave pipings, loud and clear,
Of some bird minstrel. He can sing
Of all the coming joys of spring !

THURSDAY—OCTOBER 4.

BISHOP VINCENT'S way of beginning each day was this :

I will try this day to live a simple, sincere and serene life, repelling promptly every thought of discontent, anxiety, discouragement, impurity and self-seeking ; cultivating cheerfulness, magnanimity, charity and the habit of holy silence ; exercising economy in expenditure, generosity in giving, carefulness in conversation, diligence in appointed service, fidelity in every trust, and a child-like faith in God.

FRIDAY—OCTOBER 5.

WHAT do you make of these two stories?

(a) When, in the same week, a woman saw her child killed in a street accident and her husband sent to prison, she told a friend : " I've got to keep on somehow. My husband'll need me when he comes out, and there's the baby to look after."

(b) Because her husband made an unpleasant noise when drinking his tea, his wife left him.

Perhaps neither story interests you. Or would you care to pass judgment on these two wives—after careful consideration, of course ? Is it possible that you instantly praise the first and condemn the second?

SATURDAY—OCTOBER 6.

NOW that Miss Mary has passed on, scores of boys and girls will miss those wee treats she delighted to give, for no end of children used to look in on their way to school, and to each she would give a sweet.

Yes, they'll miss Miss Mary, and the fathers and mothers of many will be thinking of her—Miss Mary gave *them* sweets, too, when they were small!

But she did more than hand out sweets—she used to smile down at the children and say : " Here's a sweet. Now run along, dear . . . and be good !"

SUNDAY—OCTOBER 7.

PRESERVE me, O God : for in Thee do I put my trust.

MONDAY—OCTOBER 8.

" FOR four years now," wrote Mr Ford, " I have been father and mother to my three young sons. The youngest hardly remembers what it's like to have a mother's love, and sometimes my eyes fill with tears when he tells me of what other boys' mums do for them.

" I'm not complaining. Some folk, kindly no doubt, suggest putting the children in a home, but could anybody do that after finding a little note like this, which was left for me one evening :—

" *Dear Dad,—There is pies and beans for your supper, and tomorrow you can have the rest of the beans for dinner with sausage. We have not been carrying on, and have got supper ready. I hope you like the place, and we have washed thoroughly. Goodnight, with lots and lots of love from your dear son Ronald. P.T.O.—Alarm is on for seven.*"

Thank you, Mr Ford, for a brave, kindly letter.

TUESDAY—OCTOBER 9.

JUST suppose for a moment that the Devil decided to go out of business !

He announced he was selling the tools of his trade —and that any of the lesser devils could buy them.

In due course the sale was held. All around his workshop the Devil had arranged Malice, Hatred, Spite, Envy, and so on—all with their price tags.

But the highest price of all wasn't for any of these. Can you guess what the Devil considered his most valuable weapon?

It was—*Discouragement*. " When you get a man down," he said, " you can do anything with him !"

And he never said a truer word.

WEDNESDAY—OCTOBER 10.

IT'S nice receiving compliments
* When you're a movie star ;*
It's nice to hear applause when you
* Have opened a bazaar.*
But, oh, the fun, the thrill, the joy—
* Beyond applause or shout—*
Of doing good so secretly
* That no one finds you out !*

THURSDAY—OCTOBER 11.

SOME friends were discussing the Pilgrim Fathers, and one man mentioned their many hardships. Then one of the ladies made a most profound statement.

" You never seem to hear about the Pilgrim Mothers. But the fact is that they put up with the same hardships—and what's more—they had to put up with the Pilgrim Fathers as well."

Could there be a hint here, gentlemen ?

FRIDAY—OCTOBER 12.

THERE was a christening in Perth, and I was there.

As we sang the hymn, " We bring them, Lord, and with the sign of sprinkled water name them Thine," four babies were carried in from the vestry.

As I sat down I gave thanks to William Robertson.

Little did I know then, he wrote the hymn in a manse still standing a few miles from where I sat !

It's just a hundred years since William Robertson brought his bride to the big stone manse at Monzievaird. As the years passed, the young couple were blessed with two boys and seven girls.

Nine times Willie Robertson christened his own children, and from his deep love for them he wrote the hymn we sang, " A little child the Saviour came."

He was only 44 when he died, but surely he left behind the blessing of a true father.

SATURDAY—OCTOBER 13.

AT the beginning of the war the Caldow home was happy . . . until, one after the other, May's father and mother and two brothers died.

It might have been the end of the world for May. But instead, through a variety of friends she secretly arranged for unhappy or needy folk to have a treat at her expense.

The other day a letter arrived for May from a prisoner in Dartmoor. He told her he, too, had lost everything in the past 20 years—indeed, that was the reason he was in prison.

To pass the time he makes fur toys, and now he asked May to accept these to give to children.

I feel this prisoner couldn't have found a happier way of atoning for whatever he did, than by bringing a smile to the face of a little child.

THE FRIENDSHIP BOOK

SUNDAY—OCTOBER 14.

I GO to prepare a place for you.

MONDAY—OCTOBER 15.

A BUSINESS acquaintance grinned at me across
a small table in a restaurant.

"You're a pretty observant chap, Francis," he
said. "Would you care to read this once and tell
me how many times the letter 'F' appears?"

As he spoke he produced a scrap of paper. I read,
"Feature films are the result of years of scientific
research combined with the experience of years."

"Most people say there are only two letter Fs."

"Must be a bit simple," I purred. "Anybody can
see there are four."

That was the signal for the man opposite to lean
back and laugh aloud. "Really, Francis," he
exclaimed. "Surely you spotted the six 'Fs.'"

When I looked again, blow me if he wasn't right !

TUESDAY—OCTOBER 16.

"LIFE'S a queer business, Mr Gay," remarked a sun-
tanned Scotsman I happened to get in conversation with in a London hotel. "A very queer thing.
For years I had one ambition : To get out of Glasgow
as soon as I could, and to get as far away as I could.
Glasgow ! Glasgow on a Sunday afternoon—nothing
to do but walk up and down Sauchiehall Street in the
rain !

"As it happened, I landed a good job in India. A
very good job. Far enough away from Scotland. All
the colour and romance of the East . . . and during the
six years I was out there the one thing I longed for was
a chance to walk up and down Sauchiehall Street in
the rain !"

WEDNESDAY—OCTOBER 17.

SHE sings while doing chores and chores.
  She keeps things clean and bright.
She mothers all her children dear,
  And tucks them up at night.
A hundred unpaid jobs are hers—
  She's busy all day long ;
She makes home, home ; she humours me,
  And smiles when things go wrong.
    How little worth there'd be in life
    Without the love of my sweet wife !

THURSDAY—OCTOBER 18.

HIS name was Ambrose Fleming and he lived in Lancashire, where his father was a minister.

A bright lad was Ambrose, and he astonished his dad one day by saying he was going to be an electrical engineer. It was rather like saying he was going to be the first man on the moon, for electricity was at that time the newest mystery. Instead, Ambrose was packed off to be a chemist.

Oh, he became a chemist all right—and a good one—but in the end, by sheer determination, he became Professor Sir Ambrose Fleming, one of the great pioneers of electricity.

There was even more than that to his determination. For years he had been troubled with deafness, and he had no patience with the ear trumpets that were the hearing aids of his day. So with his colleague, Ardente, he set about producing the very first electrical hearing aid.

Mind you, it was nothing like the modern boon which 160,000 people apply for every year. In fact, the professor's model weighed 7 lb. and had to be carried in an attache case. But it was a beginning,

It just shows what determination can do.

FRIDAY—OCTOBER 19.

EVERY now and then I take a walk with Francis Gay, and we have a heart-to-heart talk.

Does that puzzle you? Well, here's the reason.

Like you, I lead a pretty busy life ; in fact, it is hectic at times. How good, therefore, to escape from the noise and bustle and take a walk along a quiet country road and get the chance to be still, to think, and to take stock of myself.

I ask myself if I am as patient as I ought to be, as understanding, as ready to sympathise, as willing to lend a hand. I ask myself the embarrassing question—Am I practising what I preach?

I cannot say I enjoy this self-examination. But I think it serves a good purpose being alone with myself—and going back to routine feeling toned up the least bit and ready to try a bit harder to be the kind of man I'd like to be.

SATURDAY—OCTOBER 20.

AS a very young man I was terribly anxious to see my name in print in a certain very popular magazine. Time after time I submitted a story, and time after time it came back with the editor's regrets. I tried over and over again, all to no purpose. Then one day, when my mind was filled with other thoughts, the editor dropped me a line and *invited* me to write a story for him.

Since then I have over and over again discovered that in life we often batter frantically at a closed door . . . which opens easily of itself as soon as we get on with other duties.

SUNDAY—OCTOBER 21.

I AM the vine, ye are the branches.

MONDAY—OCTOBER 22.

FEELING tired, irritated and annoyed by the trivialities of life ?

Remember the old Chinese saying : " A man who cannot tolerate small ills can never accomplish great things."

TUESDAY—OCTOBER 23.

ONE of the oldest stories in the world is about King Solomon and the Queen of Sheba. According to the legend, the Queen of Sheba, having heard that Solomon was the wisest man living, paid him a visit.

Among the many gifts she took with her were two wreaths of flowers. " These," said the wily queen, " are for you. But do me a favour."

" What is it?" inquired the cautious monarch.

" Nothing much," replied the Queen. " Nothing at all for anyone as clever as you. One of these wreaths is made of artificial flowers. Tell me which is which."

For all his vast wisdom, poor King Solomon was on the horns of a dilemma. He looked from one group of flowers to the other. He touched the delicate petals and leaves and stems, and peered into the very centre of each flower—but it was no use, so skilfully had the artificial flowers been fashioned that Solomon, in all his glory, could not tell one from the other. Suddenly he had an idea. He ordered the wreaths to be carried to an open window. Presently the bees came humming round. They were attracted to one wreath. They ignored the other.

So wise King Solomon was able to answer the Queen of Sheba's riddle.

Odd, when you think of it, that the busy little bees could do what Solomon couldn't. Queer that even the cleverest people don't know everything.

WEDNESDAY—OCTOBER 24.

THE night has gathered round the house,
  The autumn wind blows cold ;
Now God be thanked for walls and roof,
  And fire of red and gold.
Although of riches I have none,
  How happy is my life ;
I envy no man anything . . .
  I've children, home and wife.

THURSDAY—OCTOBER 25.

THERE was a Gift Day at Chalmers Church, recently. A new boiler had to be paid for, so everyone was invited to bring a gift. Everyone, that is, except pensioners.

Yet nothing, it seemed, could keep those old folk from giving. One old soul handed in a £5 note she had had since Christmas. It was a present, and she'd never used it.

Another woman, aged 85, sent word for the minister to take all the money in her welfare bank into which she put a little every week. An old couple had £7 in their bank, and they gave it all.

Throughout the day gifts were gladly brought, until by 7 p.m. the kirk was richer by £330.

I don't wonder the minister made his way home with a full and a humble heart, marvelling that so many with so little could give so much.

There is an old saying that God is no man's debtor.

FRIDAY—OCTOBER 26.

IN these days he's a poor man who cannot afford now and then to give a child a shilling, but he's a poorer man who has money to spare and cannot bring himself to give any of it away.

SATURDAY—OCTOBER 27.

MRS McINNES said it with her chin up—and the Lady of the House didn't blame her. " We've never been well off," Mrs McInnes declared, " but we never wanted for anything worth having. There have been good times and bad, and I once had all four children ill when my hubby was off work, but we managed fine."

" And the secret?" my wife asked.

" Well," said Mrs McInnes, " I've always made a point of *not* spending all the money my hubby hands over—and the bit to spare piles up in a few weeks till it's a nice little reserve for emergency use. 'Tisn't easy, but well worth while !"

SUNDAY—OCTOBER 28.

BLESSED are they that hear the word of God, and keep it.

MONDAY—OCTOBER 29.

SIR, ever take your wife a cup of tea in bed?

Ever feel like calling her names—and putting on a grin instead?

Ever take home some little surprise for her?

Ever suggest the two of you go some place you're not keen on—but she likes?

Try it.

Madam, ever pretend you're tremendously interested in one of your husband's hobbies?

Ever help him with his gardening?

Ever let him hear you telling the children what a clever man their daddy is?

Ever tidy up after he's been around without telling him you've had to?

Try it.

TUESDAY—OCTOBER 30.

A YOUNG sailor called Jimmy had been brought ashore from his ship seriously ill, and it soon became clear that the only chance was a big operation.

He was in his twenties, with a ready smile and laughing eyes that twinkled even through his pain.

One evening he took a turn for the worse. It was obvious the end was near. An S O S was put out for his parents and young wife.

When they arrived they were shown to his bed—but the atmosphere round it was strangely tense. For Jimmy had married against his parents' wishes, and they had never agreed to meet the girl who became his wife. Now all three were watching the one they loved—on one side of the bed a frightened girl, and on the other a heart-broken mother and father.

Then, dramatically, the scene changed. The older woman rose, moved round to her son's wife, and put her arms about her. Not a word was spoken.

Early next day Jimmy died, and perhaps the last thing he saw on this earth was his mother's arms around his wife. But how pitifully true it is that quite often it needs the death of a loved one to heal a family quarrel.

WEDNESDAY—OCTOBER 31.

Do a bit of kindness—
Get a lot of fun.
Share a neighbour's sorrow—
You'll be glad you've done.
Lend a hand to someone—
They'll help you one day.
Make somebody happy—
Life for you is gay.
Give away yourself—you bet
Wealth of joy you're bound to get !

NOVEMBER

WHO can tell what manner of man a boy will grow
to be?

When Davie Douglas was young he was such a
high-spirited handful his schoolmistress despatched
him to another school, where there was a man in
charge ! Davie was tamed there, but never broken.

In time he became a gardener whose love of every
growing thing took him thousands of miles from home.
He used his boundless energy and courage to explore
the farthest reaches of the great Columbia River in
Canada in his search for new trees and plants that
would grow in Britain.

Alas, Davie was only 35 when he was killed in an
accident, and his promising career was cut short.

It was Davie who found and sent to us such delights
as the flowering currant, Californian poppy, berberis,
clarkia, nemophilia, and the blue lupin that is one of
the parents of all our lupins—not forgetting the stately
Douglas fir in our forests.

He won no statue, but in countless gardens he wins
the unspoken thanks of all who share his love of
nature's beauty.

I LIKE the story of little Pauline who simply would
not go to sleep. When all else failed, her grandfather lay down on top of the bed beside her and
pretended he was going to sleep. So Pauline lay
down too, and was very still and quiet.

Quarter of an hour later her parents were
astonished to see the living-room door open and
Pauline walk in. " It's all right," she said, quite
happily. " I've got grandpa off to sleep at last !"

A BIT BIG!

If you want a pet to fondle
The wolfhound you should ban,
For when he takes the notion
He gets up and pats the man!

DAVID HOPE

EVENING

The shadows lengthen and a breeze
  Comes blowing from the ben.
Proud from feats on crag and corrie
  Come home the climbing men.

The burns take up their ancient tune
  Old ere man was known.
The dark comes pouring down the hills
  And night reclaims her own.

DAVID HOPE

WISHES

It's nice if we can own a train,
*   A diamond bracelet or a yacht,*
But better still if we can find
*   A joy in things we HAVEN'T got.*

DAVID HOPE

SATURDAY—NOVEMBER 3.

A FRIEND sent me these challenging lines :—

> *I never cut my neighbour's throat ;*
> *My neighbour's gold I never stole ;*
> *I never spoiled his house or land—*
> *But God have mercy on my soul.*
> *For I am haunted night and day*
> *By all the things I have not done ;*
> *Of unattempted loveliness*
> *And costly valour never won !*

SUNDAY—NOVEMBER 4.

IN My Father's house are many mansions.

MONDAY—NOVEMBER 5.

DR MACFARLANE is, if I may say so, a busy man. Recently, Mrs Emily Hislop walked into his surgery, her brow furrowed with worry. You see, for 15 years she has wanted to go to America to visit her sister, who has promised to pay all expenses.

But Mrs Hislop suffers from bronchitis, and whether or not it's because of this, she hasn't been able to get a visa to enter the U.S.A.

The doctor listened in silence. But when Mrs Hislop had gone he set to work. He wrote letters . . . and phoned . . . and in doing so he worked a small miracle. For when Mrs Hislop answered a knock on the door the other day she found her minister standing on the steps with the wonderful news he had from Dr MacFarlane—her visa had at last been granted ! No wonder tears of joy streamed down her face.

Yes, it's wonderful what a helping hand can sometimes mean. For, remember, in fifteen minutes Dr MacFarlane accomplished something that a poor widow had been trying to do for fifteen years.

TUESDAY—NOVEMBER 6.

THE minister and his wife had both been ill, and at the end of the minister's first service after their recovery, one of the church elders offered a prayer of thanksgiving for their safe recovery.

" O Lord," he said, " we thank Thee for bringing safely back to us our beloved minister and his dear wife. Lord, Thou carest for man and beast."

Had you been the minister's wife would you have been offended? Or would you have had sense enough to know that words mean nothing, the spirit everything?

WEDNESDAY—NOVEMBER 7.

THEY laughed and sang and loved, those lads
  Who died that we might live;
And, splendid in their manly prime,
  Gave all they had to give.
God give us grace and righteous pride
  To live as finely as they died !

THURSDAY—NOVEMBER 8.

WHY didn't he say : " This is the end ? "

He had money, brilliance, fame, dynamic energy, till one day, shortly before he was forty, he was stricken with polio. He became a helpless cripple. He wore elaborate and clumsy harness. He was dependent on the help of nurses. He leaned on a stick . . . and there was no possibility of ever being the athletic figure he had once been.

Could you have blamed him for giving up the fight, becoming a spectator only, lying back and cursing ? But Franklin Delano Roosevelt kept on and on, battling away . . . and won lasting fame as one of the greatest Presidents the U.S.A. has known.

FRIDAY—NOVEMBER 9.

LORD, bless all little children. Do Thou guide their unsteady feet. Do Thou protect them from harm. Preserve them in their tender years. And help us, Lord, to be what we ought to be with children in our care. May our lips be clean. Let us so live that we may never cause one of them to stumble ; so act that we may never wound one little life ; so humbly walk that they may keep in step with us, looking up to us in the assurance that we will bring them to a happy place.

SATURDAY—NOVEMBER 10.

IT happened on the heaving deck of a landing-craft on the eve of D-Day.

The air was tense with waiting, and the padre, the Rev. W. Vine Russell, wondered whether he would conduct a service that night—for he knew the men who thronged the vessel had much on their minds. Yet as he went on deck, first one, then another, then more and more soldiers and sailors came forward.

It was to be a Communion service, and as Mr Russell saw how many were anxious to take part he knew his own Communion vessels would never cope with the crowd on deck.

What then was to be done? He didn't know, but he began the service just the same.

Then, even as he spoke the words " . . . this do in remembrance of Me . . ." a burly Commando drew a chipped enamelled tea mug from his pack.

All over the deck other mugs appeared, and the wine was reverently poured from one to the other.

Many of those who landed on the beaches never came back, yet surely they went forward strong in the strength that can come only from an inner steadfastness.

SUNDAY—NOVEMBER 11.

I AM the resurrection, and the life : he that believeth on Me, though he die, yet shall he live : And whosoever liveth and believeth on Me shall never die.

MONDAY—NOVEMBER 12.

WHO was William Edward Hickson ?

It's more than likely you don't know—and, frankly, there isn't much reason why you should know anything. All I know is that he was an English writer, born in 1803, who died in 1870. Except one other thing . . . a very important thing ; for he has left behind four lines of poetry which challenge each of us, and may shame us in moments of cowardice and defeat to battle on more bravely.

For it was William Edward Hickson who wrote :—

'Tis a lesson you should heed,
Try, try again ;
If at first you don't succeed,
Try, try again !

TUESDAY—NOVEMBER 13.

FOR weeks he had put pennies and small pieces of silver in his money box. Now the thrilling moment had come. The red tin box was taken down from the shelf and the little fellow eagerly unlocked it. Out came the hoard of money, and it was counted —fourteen shillings and fivepence !

" Why !" exclaimed the owner of the fortune, " I never thought I should get out so much."

" You wouldn't," said his father, " if you hadn't put so much in."

And it's the same with living, isn't it ? Those who put most in get most out !

WEDNESDAY—NOVEMBER 14.

A HAPPY smile from you might make
  Some anxious heart rejoice ;
You don't know how some lonely soul
  Might thrill to hear your voice !

THURSDAY—NOVEMBER 15.

PHILOSOPHERS all down the ages have observed impressively that mankind is much the same in all lands and in all ages, but I think little Gertrude Cheney sums it all up brilliantly for us. When only nine she wrote this startling and humiliating sentence :—

All people are made alike. They are made of bones, flesh and dinners. Only the dinners are different.

FRIDAY—NOVEMBER 16.

COULD you put into one word one of the chief characteristics of our time? I think I can. It is the word *get*.

The thought occurs to me that our newspapers would read rather oddly if for a week, say, the captions were all about people who wanted to *give!*

For, although the getters usually get the headlines, it's the givers who are keeping society together.

It is those who *give* who bless—the thinkers and poets, the gardeners and the musicians, the doctors and nurses, kindly, friendly, neighbourly people who, even if paid to do their job, go far beyond it.

The getters are never happy—they are bound to be miserable if they haven't got all they want ; and the givers are never really unhappy, for the more folk they bless and enrich and help and cheer and comfort, the happier they are.

THE FRIENDSHIP BOOK

SATURDAY—NOVEMBER 17.

JUST to show that the dictionary is not always right, did you know that :—

An alarm clock is a device for adults who have no children to wake them?

A childish game is one at which your wife beats you?

Diplomacy is the art of letting someone have your own way?

Football is a game played between two teams, with a ball and about twenty thousand referees?

Summer is the season when the children slam the doors they left open all winter?

SUNDAY—NOVEMBER 18.

IN your patience ye shall win your souls.

MONDAY—NOVEMBER 19.

HAVE you heard the story of the man who called to see the minister recently? The minister did not know his visitor, but asked him in, and then said, " Now, what can I do for you?"

" Well," was the reply, " I'd like to know if I can join your church."

The minister stared. "Why do you want to join *my* church?" he demanded.

" Well," said the visitor, " I work in a factory, and the chap at the machine next to mine used to be the meanest man I knew, as well as the laziest and the most dishonest ; but since his wife got him to attend your church he's become altogether changed, and he won't rest till I come along with him. I thought I ought to ask you first, though. My workmate's a different chap nowadays . . . I'd like to be a bit more like him."

TUESDAY—NOVEMBER 20.

IT was an unpleasant morning, grey and depressing
with a cold wind and a wretched drizzle of rain.
Then, about eleven, the sun came out.

What a transformation. At once the air felt more
genial. There was a widening patch of blue in the
sky. The pavements began to dry up, and the people
hurrying up and down were more cheerful.

Have you ever asked yourself what you are—
meteorologically speaking? When you join a group
of people do you bring with you a pleasant or a
depressing atmosphere?

Are you like a fog which makes us all wretched—
or like the sun, cheering up, enheartening us, showing
us all up in our best colours?

WEDNESDAY—NOVEMBER 21.

WHEN the world is kind and when fair the day,
It is easy then to be bright and gay.
May God grant that you in the darkest night
Will be filled with strength to be gay and bright.

THURSDAY—NOVEMBER 22.

HOW can you be *sure* when you get up in the
morning that you'll sleep soundly at bedtime ?

You can't. But you can be very nearly certain if
you remember this ; the day challenges you to do
what needs to be done. If you do what you ought to
do, and do it well without a lot of fuss or any
complaint, if you do it with all your heart and soul,
and as cheerily as you can—even if you hate it—
depend on it, when bedtime comes you'll sleep like a
top !

It's mostly the duty dodgers who have restless
nights.

FRIDAY—NOVEMBER 23.

AT first sight you'd think the little church was like any other church.

The minister is in his pulpit. The opening hymn has been announced. Row upon row of men and women stand in the pews, their hymnaries open, their eyes intent on the first line, or on the pulpit. Their praise begins . . . yet not a sound is heard.

Only the voice of the minister breaks the silence as he reads the hymn and, with amazing agility, his hands and fingers also spell out every word to the final Amen.

It is the same with the readings, prayers and sermon for, of course, this is the church for the deaf and dumb.

I doubt if any service is more moving in its simplicity, or any silence so eloquent.

SATURDAY—NOVEMBER 24.

FOR 35 years Mr Rae has been almost stone deaf. He was totally deaf in one ear, and the hearing was gradually going in the other.

It is terribly difficult for any of us to face a future in which we're cut off from all the familiar sounds of life, but to Mr Rae it was a prospect that was even harder to bear, for he was a church organist who loved beautiful music.

Then one day Mr Rae heard of a faith-healing service. Many and many a time he had heard the words—" thy faith hath made thee whole." Could his faith help him, he wondered?

Well, he went to the service. The preacher held his hands over Mr Rae's ears and asked that he might be cured. Wonderful to relate, as the preacher took his hands away, Mr Rae realised he could hear, yes, even a whisper!

Friends, you never know what the next day can bring in happiness, do you?

SUNDAY—NOVEMBER 25.

WHILE ye have the light, believe on the light.

MONDAY—NOVEMBER 26.

I LIKE the story of the great Joseph Lister, the eminent surgeon. Coming out of the operating theatre, where he had just performed a major operation, he met a little girl, a patient in the hospital, who asked him to operate on her doll. He did. He sewed it up for her, so that the stuffing wouldn't come out. He was a great man—great not only because he revolutionised surgery, but because nothing was too small for him to do.

TUESDAY—NOVEMBER 27.

WHEN Sir Harry Lauder was struggling to make his way as a comedian, he met a young man, Willie Blackwood, and one week-end Willie asked Harry to go home with him and meet his family.

They all sat together for supper, with Willie's father at the top of the table. Soon everyone was laughing at Harry's yarns. But when he told a story that might have been in slightly doubtful taste Mr Blackwood excused himself, rose from the table, and asked Harry if he would come to his study later.

When Harry duly went, Mr Blackwood said slowly and kindly, " Young man, you have the power to become a great comedian and an ambassador for the Scots—if you use your true humour and talent. But never rely on less than the best. . . ."

Many years later, when, as Sir Harry Lauder, his name was a household word, he thanked Mr Blackwood for the good counsel that had helped to guide him.

It takes a big man to accept advice—and a bigger man to acknowledge its worth.

WEDNESDAY—NOVEMBER 28.

THE days are drawing in, and now
The darker nights have come.
And after dark the stay-at-homes
May feel a little glum.
And yet, how nice when wails the storm
To keep a friendly fire warm !

THURSDAY—NOVEMBER 29.

I DON'T want to frighten you, but I want to warn you that if you are a father or a mother you are being watched !

Take care ! You are being watched—not by a villain, but by a child. What you are now, remember, determines in large measure what your child will be in twenty years' time.

Be careful !

FRIDAY—NOVEMBER 30.

I'M thinking of Mrs Moran, a dear old soul so troubled with arthritis in her legs that even getting about her house is a painful business.

She uses a chair to sit on while she prepares her meals. She cannot sew or knit because of arthritis in her fingers. She has no one of her own to visit her, and no radio. And, incredible as it may seem, she hasn't been out of her house for 21 years !

A depressing life, you might say. Yet I can't think of a brighter spirit or a more contented one than Mrs Moran. Simply because she never learned how to be sorry for herself. . . .

Friends, I don't know the secret of Mrs Moran's contentment, but as I look around this restless old world I only wish many of us knew its priceless blessing.

DECEMBER

LIFE is a building. It rises slowly day by day throughout the years. Every new lesson we learn lays a block on the edifice which is rising silently within us. Every experience, every touch of another life on ours, every influence that impresses us, every book we read, every conversation we have, every act of our commonest days adds something to the invisible building.

ONE only is the Lawgiver and Judge, even He who is able to save and to destroy : but who art thou that judgest thy neighbour?

DOUGLAS BURNS was happily married with six lovely children, and everything in the world to look forward to.

Then suddenly he was struck down by a form of polio.

There was only one hope left . . . prayer.

The minister prayed, Mrs Burns and the children prayed, his friends prayed, and Douglas himself tried to offer his own silent prayer.

Then, just as suddenly, a few days later there was a sharp pain in Douglas's right leg—a pain where there was supposed to be no feeling at all ! The doctors knew then that all would be well.

Today Douglas is back home, and he will soon be his old self again. Do you wonder he believes prayers for him were answered, and that he is today the walking proof ?

TUESDAY—DECEMBER 4.

NO wonder the doctor was worried.

Britain was in the grip of a grim depression Money was short, so, of course, the flow of donations that kept Dr Barnardo's Homes going had dried up and almost stopped. Now, with a bank overdraft of £20,000 and five thousand children to care for, the position couldn't have looked bleaker.

What could the good doctor do? He went into his office, closed the door, and knelt beside his desk in prayer. No one knows how long he stayed there, but when he rose he felt compelled to write the story of his five thousand orphans.

A firm of printers offered to print two million copies of it, and other firms addressed two million envelopes. The leaflets were posted to folk all over the country. Even the cost of posting was guaranteed by a friend.

Believe it or not, only two days later six postal vans drew up at Dr Barnardo's office laden with cheques, postal orders, stamps, gifts and offers of help.

So through this remarkable act of faith not only was the day saved, but the debt was wiped out, and Dr Barnardo was able to start again.

You know, friends, it reminds me of another story about a hungry five thousand. . . .

WEDNESDAY—DECEMBER 5.

I'VE often asked the Lord to bless
My child and make him good ;
I've always trusted Him, and felt
My prayers were understood.
Yet how my heart was touched last night
When little Ian said—
" Please, God, don't let my Mum get cross,
But make her smile instead."

THE FRIENDSHIP BOOK

THURSDAY—DECEMBER 6.

" WHAT sort of a man was he?" I asked.

My friend couldn't tell me the age of the man in question, and he didn't describe his appearance or income or position. All he said was, " Well, he was this sort of man—he always raised his hat when he met the charlady who washed the office floor."

Is there much more I need to know of him?

FRIDAY—DECEMBER 7.

THE doors of a ward in Little Cairnie Hospital, Arbroath, swung open, and two young men marched in, their faces wreathed in smiles.

They went straight to the bed in the corner. With a bow they greeted the old woman who lay there, wished her many happy returns of the day, and handed over a gift. After a chat they got up, patted her hand—and they were off again !

Who were they, you ask? They were two members of the Arbroath Round Table Club—a band of young men who are surely knights in the truest sense of the word. For they have adopted not just one patient, but every one in Little Cairnie Hospital, a place where old folk are cared for.

For ten years now they have remembered the birthdays of everybody there. They see that a card is sent off, they buy a wee present—and on the great day two of the young men go out specially to Little Cairnie to hand it over and wish a surprised and grateful old soul " Happy Birthday."

As I say, they're a band of ordinary young men, from all sorts of jobs and from all walks of life. But if the original knights of the round table were any more gallant than these modern knights—even if they don't wear shining armour—Francis Gay will have pleasure in eating his hat !

SATURDAY—DECEMBER 8.

THE farmer looked at his farmhand at breakfast.
" Bill," he said, " I've been up half the night.
I've never heard it blow harder and I was sure those
stacks nearest the stable would have their thatch
carried off. I couldn't sleep for thinking about them.
Didn't the wind keep you awake?"

" No," said Bill.

" But weren't you worried about those stacks?"

" No. You see, I thatched them myself."

SUNDAY—DECEMBER 9.

I AM the living bread which came down out of
heaven.

MONDAY—DECEMBER 10.

FOR some weeks a little boy had often cried himself
to sleep because he was worried about his
mummy, who was ill.

Maybe it was the way she looked and spoke, because
Daddy was dead and mother and son were very close.
Maybe it was only his imagination.

Even so, the worry grew so strong that he asked—
" You're not going to die, are you, Mummy?

" You promised you wouldn't die till I was grown
up and able to look after myself," went on the little
boy, growing bolder.

His mother stroked his hair. " I remember," she
said. " And I promise . . ."

Alas, it was a promise she could not keep . . . she
passed away in her sleep.

Now I hope with all my heart that whoever broke
the news to that little boy touched the heights of
gentleness, for it was a moment that will be
engraved on his mind for the rest of his life.

TUESDAY—DECEMBER 11.

I CAN only guess what young Robert Foster was thinking. . . .

It was in 1945 that Robert was taken to Quarrier's Homes at Bridge of Weir—a baby only eight weeks old. The war was not yet finished, but inside the warmth and love of Quarrier's the strife-torn world was far away.

For sixteen years it was the only home this orphan laddie ever knew. And then he reached the moment that comes to nearly every one of us some time or other—he was leaving home to step out into the world. He was going to sea.

As he made his way to the front door he remembered all the happiness he had known, the " parents " he had loved as his own and who had loved him in return. Suddenly his collar seemed too tight, and his eyes blurred. . . .

He took a tighter grip of his case, which held enough clothes to do him for two years, and his bankbook with the nest egg that had been started for him.

But, of course, the most precious gift of all wasn't in his case, it was in his heart and soul . . . the gift of character.

Surely no one, orphan or no, can set out into the world with a better gift than that.

WEDNESDAY—DECEMBER 12.

THERE'S such a lot in this bad old world
    To make us angry or sad,
So many people or things which just
    Send sensible folk quite mad.
Cool down a bit, and you'll quickly find
    There are lovely things galore,
And friendly folk, and a wealth of joy
    We ought to be thankful for !

THURSDAY—DECEMBER 13.

THURSDAY night wouldn't be the same at Knowe Park Hospital without George Temple—and I'll tell you why.

Nearly ten years ago George first went there to visit an old, old friend. And what a faithful visitor he was. Not a week passed for three years but he was at his friend's bedside.

Then, alas, his old friend died and George sadly took his leave of Matron, thanking her for allowing him so many visits. That would be the last of him now, he said.

But it wasn't to be. "There are still other old people here, you know, Mr Temple," the matron said gently. It was a challenge George couldn't refuse. "Right," he said, "I'll come on Thursday."

And every Thursday night he has kept his promise.

He goes from bed to bed, bringing some of the outside chat and cheer that means so much to invalids. Sometimes, too, he holds a little service, and it would do your heart good to see how much the old folk enjoy it all.

A small ministry, you might think. But I don't think many will beat that for good works!

FRIDAY—DECEMBER 14.

LORD, help us to win little conquests. It is sometimes easy to steel our hearts against great shocks, to bear terrible pains, to face tremendous odds, to rush into the thick of the fight, and do amazing things; but help us to accomplish small things with a splendid grace. Teach us to remain calm when trifling annoyances might so easily ruffle us, to keep our temper over petty affairs, to be great enough not to worry about little everyday matters which fray our nerves and make us over-anxious.

SATURDAY—DECEMBER 15.

YES," said the cheery little lady, " it's nice having neighbours who keep popping in to borrow something !"

" I wouldn't have thought of it that way," said I.

" Oh, but it's true," she replied. " It's thrilling when you're on such good terms with folk that they just shout over the wall, or look in at the door, and feel that they know you well enough to borrow something. It makes you feel so useful, you know, and, of course, you can't be lonely !"

SUNDAY—DECEMBER 16.

WHAT doth it profit, my brethren, if a man say he hath faith, but have not works? Can that faith save him?

MONDAY—DECEMBER 17.

ONE Sunday evening, the Rev. Peter Brodie set out for church in his car, but only two hundred yards from the manse the car spluttered and stopped . . . . the petrol tank was empty.

As the road ran downhill to the nearest garage, there was just a chance he could coast most of the way.

But first he needed a push. In a twinkling this was supplied by a lady in a new hat and Sunday-best, who urged on her two young sons to combine forces with her and push! Slowly the car gathered speed, but, alas, it eased to a halt again.

Just then a police sergeant got it rolling again.

Now only one obstacle remained—a halt sign. But the sergeant realised this. He sped on ahead on his bicycle, stopped the traffic, and waved Mr Brodie through so that he free-wheeled with royal-like privilege towards the garage and petrol!

TUESDAY—DECEMBER 18.

OVER one hundred years ago a Swiss man, Henry Dunant, was travelling through Northern Italy at the time war was raging between Austria and France. When he arrived at Castiglione he found that many dead and wounded were lying in the gutter.

He could have passed by on the other side for, after all, he was from another country and had no part in the war. Instead, he banded the villagers together, commandeered the church hall as a hospital, and gently bore the suffering and dying through its doors. Then off he went to bring in more wounded.

But when he arrived at the hall he saw two soldiers being turned out, although they were gravely ill. He asked why they weren't being attended to. " They're the enemy. They're not on our side !"

" Take them in again !" Dunant commanded. " All men are brothers !"

From that moment he devoted his life to forming an organisation to look after the wounded on all battlefields.

As a tribute to its founder, the headquarters of the movement were built in Switzerland, and the colours of the Swiss flag (a white cross on a red background) were reversed to give the best-known emblem in the world—the Red Cross.

WEDNESDAY—DECEMBER 19.

TAKE her flowers, fruit or sweets,
  Granny's glad of these ;
Lives alone, and well turned eighty—
  Never hard to please.
But there's one thing she likes better
  Than a gift from you :
Someone looking in to see her,
  Someone to talk to !

THURSDAY—DECEMBER 20.

AN American Army recruit was raking a path at headquarters when a man in uniform strolled past. " Hey, pal," the recruit said, " give me a light, will you?" The stranger obliged and started to walk on.

Another soldier dashed up and whispered to the recruit, " Don't you know who that is? That's the General !"

With sinking heart the recruit ran after the General to apologise. " I'm sorry, sir," he said. " I've only been in the army two days and all the uniforms look alike to me."

" That's all right," replied the General with a broad grin. " Only take my advice. Never try it on a second lieutenant !"

FRIDAY—DECEMBER 21.

THE Lady of the House took me into a big store. We were there—with several thousand other folk—an hour or so, and at last battled our way out of the glare into the fog as the winter day came to an end.

" You meet all sorts in a store," remarked the Lady of the House, fresh as ever after the ordeal.

" You get bumped and pushed," I muttered.

But she went on pleasantly—evidently thinking as she spoke : " You know, darling, I'm sure it's true that the less people have to spend the more they enjoy it. I've seen a lady buying a fur coat, and I've seen two small girls trying to spend a shilling or two on something for Mum ! The first was rather bored. The children were excited."

I nodded. " I hope you didn't give the little girls anything," said I, frowning terribly.

The Lady of the House beamed. " Not a penny," said she. " But I saw *you* give them something !"

SATURDAY—DECEMBER 22.

I SAW a wonderful picture the other morning. It wasn't in an art gallery, nor was it painted by a famous artist. It was framed in a cottage doorway. A young mother gathered up her little son who had fallen and hurt his knee. She comforted him and " kissed him better " and dried his tears.

A wonderful picture in an ordinary frame.

SUNDAY—DECEMBER 23.

AND they came into the house and saw the young Child with Mary His mother ; and they fell down and worshipped Him ; and opening their treasures they offered unto Him gifts, gold and frankincense and myrrh.

MONDAY—DECEMBER 24.

DURING the war Mr Clark was in Hong Kong, and when the Japanese took possession of the city he and his family were thrown into Stanley Prison.

Three years later they were still there, and he will never forget Christmas Day of 1944. There was no light in the prison—not even a candle. It was cold and cheerless. Their Christmas dinner was a coarse cake made from rice they had saved.

All at once from a cell nearby came the sound of the old carol, " Silent Night." A hush fell over the building, and the soft, clear song, sung by a band of Russian P.O.W.s, echoed down the long corridors. Mr Clark felt the tears run down his cheeks, and he realised that even there, in prison, it was truly Christmas.

That night, for a time at least, all thoughts of hunger and cold, bitterness and strife, were forgotten, and the spirit of Christmas filled the hearts of the men and women as it does the world over.

TUESDAY—DECEMBER 25.

STRANGE that I hadn't heard before of the magic Christmas tree.

It stands each year in a big room at the Royal Victoria School in Newcastle. Its spreading branches are gay with tinsel and decorations, laden with presents, and right on top is the fairy, wand in hand.

All around stand the children in their party best . . . their faces are alight with happiness and all eyes are turned towards the beautiful tree . . . the tree they cannot see, for every child there is blind.

Suddenly, noiselessly, the fairy lights are switched on and the tree shines in all its glory. Then an amazing thing happens. The very instant the lights are lit, a long sigh of delight comes from every child!

Mr Bernard Best, headmaster of the school, tells me that every year visitors are taken aback by the spontaneous " OOH !" of his blind children when their tree lights up. And it is a moment that never fails to touch him as he looks around the little faces that glow in their own darkness.

But Mr Best can no more explain than I can how it is that blind children gasp with joy when their Christmas tree lights up.

Perhaps only the fairy knows, for I'm sure it all has something to do with the magic of Christmas.

WEDNESDAY—DECEMBER 26.

LORD, give me gentleness that I
A friendly soul may be,
And always think of others first,
That they may see in me
Some hint of that compassion which
Descended from above
When Christ came down at Christmas time
To teach us how to love.

THURSDAY—DECEMBER 27.

A FRIEND, writing a cheery letter from his bed, tells me the news, asks how I am, sends his kindest regards to the Lady of the House, and adds—
" Keep cheery, Francis ! Never mind if the roof falls in as long as you and your wife don't fall out !"

I liked that. It's not only neat—it's sound. The truth is, a terrible lot of misfortune can come your way and leave you little the worse as long as you and your wife face it bravely together, and remain faithful and devoted in fair weather and foul.

Let the roof fall in—who cares? What does it really matter as long as husband and wife don't fall out?

FRIDAY—DECEMBER 28.

I KNEW George Home. In 1915, as a young man of 20, he joined the navy, and two years later, as a result of war service, he had to go to hospital. I don't know if he realised it then—but he was to spend the rest of his life there.

At first George could still get about on sticks, and until 1939 he was able to move around in his chair. But as the years passed he had to spend more time in bed, until he could hardly even move a finger.

He read, of course—but he was so helpless he couldn't turn the pages. He liked his smoke, too—so one of the male nurses rigged up an ingenious affair of bobbins and string, to hold the cigarette.

Thus life was bearable, and all the time I knew George he faced it with the courage he showed when he was a young sailor in the war. Then, when he was 65 years old, George passed quietly away. At his funeral service his friends sang the 23rd Psalm as a last tribute to the man who lived so long and so bravely in the valley of the shadow.

SATURDAY—DECEMBER 29.

IT is almost midnight on the last day of December, 1944. In a little farmhouse an elderly couple stand ready to leave for the watch-night service in the kirk.

Just then the phone bell rings. The elderly farmer crosses the room and lifts the receiver. A voice speaks . . . the farmer starts in disbelief, and with tears in his eyes he turns to his wife and tells her to listen.

It was their son who was calling—the Rev. Donald Caskie, of the Scots Kirk in Paris—the minister who became known as the Tartan Pimpernel.

For years his mother and father did not know whether he was dead or alive. They only hoped—and prayed. Now he was actually speaking to them—almost like a voice from the dead.

There couldn't be a happier start to a New Year.

SUNDAY—DECEMBER 30.

GRACE to you and peace be multiplied in the knowledge of God and of Jesus our Lord.

MONDAY—DECEMBER 31.

THE year grows old. Isn't this time to look back?

There are two ways of doing it. You can look back at the shadows and feel bitter or resentful. You can do this very easily—and the result will be you will begin the year with a bad grace.

You can, if you choose, recall the sunshine.

How heart-warming it is to remember the happy things the year has brought—the neighbourliness, gifts which have come your way, gentle words which have cheered you, scenes you delight to bring to mind, countless little joys.

There is an old saying which bids us, *Think, and thank God.* Isn't this the time for that?

Where The Photographs Were Taken

HILLSIDE CHURCH — *Kilmorich Church, Argyll.*

THE KEY — *Watergate Row, Chester.*

WEAPONS — *Harlech Castle, Merioneth.*

A WINTER WALK — *Lade Braes, St Andrews.*

THE BUILDERS — *Dunfermline Abbey.*

THE RIVER'S SONG — *Ganllwyd Valley, Merioneth.*

THE LEGIONS OF SPRING — *Dunton, Beds.*

THE LITTLE ROADS — *Seil Sound, Argyll.*

THE DAY'S WORK — *Gravesend.*

IN PRAISE OF DUCKS — *Aberffraw, Anglesey.*

TAKE YOUR TIME — *Great King's Hill, Bucks.*

THE FIRST TIME I ——! — *River Quaich, Perthshire.*

BOUNTY — *Loch Creran, Argyll.*

THE SUN IN TOWN — *Trafalgar Square, London.*

GOLDEN MOMENTS — *Monreith, Wigtownshire.*

* IN THE PARK — *St Stephens Green, Dublin.*

THE HILLMAN'S WISH — *Glenisla, Angus.*

EVENING — *Glencoe, Argyll.*

* *By courtesy of the Irish Tourist Association.*

Printed and Published in Great Britain by D. C. Thomson & Co., Ltd., and John Leng & Co., Ltd., London, Glasgow, Manchester and Dundee.